Financial and Accounting Guide for Not-for-Profit Organizations

NONPROFIT LAW, FINANCE, AND MANAGEMENT SERIES

The Art of Planned Giving: Understanding Donors and the Culture of Giving by Douglas E. White

Charity, Advocacy, and the Law by Bruce R. Hopkins

The Complete Guide to Nonprofit Management by Smith, Bucklin & Associates

Developing Affordable Housing: A Practical Guide for Nonprofit Organizations by Bennett L. Hecht

Financial and Accounting Guide for Not-for-Profit Organizations, Fifth Edition by Malvern J. Gross, Jr., Richard F. Larkin, Roger S. Bruttomesso, John J. McNally, Price Waterhouse LLP

Fund-Raising Cost Effectiveness: A Self-Assessment Workbook by James M. Greenfield

Fund-Raising: Evaluating and Managing the Fund Development Process by James M. Greenfield

Fund-Raising Fundamentals: A Guide to Annual Giving for Professionals and Volunteers by James M. Greenfield

Fund-Raising Regulation: A State-by-State Handbook of Registration Forms, Requirements, and Procedures by Seth Perlman and Betsy Hills Bush

Fund-Raising Regulation Report by Bruce R. Hopkins and Betsy Hills Bush

The Law of Fund-Raising, Second Edition by Bruce R. Hopkins

The Law of Tax-Exempt Healthcare Organizations by Thomas K. Hyatt and Bruce R. Hopkins

The Law of Tax-Exempt Organizations, Sixth Edition by Bruce R. Hopkins

A Legal Guide to Starting and Managing a Nonprofit Organization, Second Edition by Bruce R. Hopkins

Managing Affordable Housing: A Practical Guide to Creating Stable Communities by Bennett L. Hecht, Local Initiatives Support Coalition, Inc., and James Stockard

The Legal Answer Book for Nonprofit Managers by Bruce R. Hopkins

The Nonprofit Counsel by Bruce R. Hopkins

The Nonprofit Law Dictionary by Bruce R. Hopkins

Nonprofit Litigation: A Practical Guide with Forms and Checklists by Steve Bachmann

The Nonprofit Management Handbook: Operating Policies and Procedures by Tracy Daniel Connors

The Nonprofit Manager's Resource Dictionary by Ronald A. Landskroner

Nonprofit Organizations' Business Forms: Disk Edition by John Wiley & Sons, Inc.

Partnerships and Joint Ventures Involving Tax-Exempt Organizations by Michael I. Sanders

Planned Giving: Management, Marketing, and Law by Ronald R. Jordan and Katelyn L. Quynn

Reengineering Your Nonprofit Organization: A Guide to Strategic Transformation by Alceste T. Pappas

Reinventing the University: Managing and Financing Institutions of Higher Education by Sandra L. Johnson and Sean C. Rush, Coopers & Lybrand, L.L.P.

Streetsmart Financial Basics for Nonprofit Managers by Thomas A. McLaughlin

Successful Marketing Strategies for Nonprofit Organizations by Barry J. McLeish

The Tax Law of Charitable Giving by Bruce R. Hopkins

Tax Planning and Compliance for Tax-Exempt Organizations: Forms, Checklists, Procedures, Second Edition by Jody Blazek

The Volunteer Management Handbook by Tracy Daniel Connors

Financial and Accounting Guide for Not-for-Profit Organizations

Fifth Edition

1996 Supplement

Malvern J. Gross, Jr., CPA
Retired Partner, Price Waterhouse LLP
Richard F. Larkin, CPA
Director, Price Waterhouse LLP
Roger S. Bruttomesso, CPA
Chairman, Not-for-Profit Industry Services Group, Price Waterhouse LLP
John J. McNally, CPA
Retired Partner, Price Waterhouse LLP

John Wiley & Sons, Inc.

New York • Chichester • Brisbane • Toronto • Singapore

This text is printed on acid-free paper.

This publication is designed to provide accurate and authoritative information in regard to the subject matter covered. It is sold with the understanding that the publisher is not engaged in rendering legal, accounting, or other professional services. If legal advice or other expert assistance is required, the services of a competent professional person should be sought.

Library of Congress Cataloging in Publication Data:

Gross, Malvern J.
Financial and accounting guide for not-for-profit organizations / Malvern J. Gross, Richard F. Larkin.—5th ed.
p. cm.—(Nonprofit law, finance, and management series)
Includes bibliographical references and index.
ISBN 0-471-10474-4 (alk. paper)
ISBN 0-471-14037-6 (supplement)
1. Nonprofit organizations—Accounting. I. Larkin, Richard F.
II. Title. III. Series.
HF5686.N56G76 1995
657'.98—dc20 94-33767

Printed in the United States of America

10 9 8 7 6 5 4 3 2 1

SUBSCRIPTION NOTICE

This Wiley product is updated on a periodic basis with supplements to reflect important changes in the subject matter. If you purchased this product directly from John Wiley & Sons, Inc., we have already recorded your subscription for this update service.

If, however, you purchased this product from a bookstore and wish to receive (1) the current update at no additional charge, and (2) future updates and revised or related volumes billed separately with a 30-day examination review, please send your name, company name (if applicable), address, and the title of the product to:

Supplement Department
John Wiley & Sons, Inc.
One Wiley Drive
Somerset, NJ 08875
1-800-225-5945

For customers outside the United States, please contact the Wiley office nearest you:

Professional & Reference Division
John Wiley & Sons Canada, Ltd.
22 Worcester Road
Rexdale, Ontario M9W 1L1
(416) 675-3580
1-800-567-4797
FAX (416) 675-6599

John Wiley & Sons, Ltd.
Baffins Lane
Chicester
West Sussex, PO19 1UD
UNITED KINGDOM
(44) (243) 779777

Jarcaranda Wiley Ltd.
PRT Division
P.O. Box 174
North Ryde, NSW 2113
AUSTRALIA
(02) 805-1100
FAX (02) 805-1597

John Wiley & Sons (SEA) Pte. Ltd.
37 Jalan Pemimpin
Block B #05-04
Union Industrial Building
SINGAPORE 2057
(65) 258-1157

About the Authors

Malvern J. Gross, Jr. is a retired partner of Price Waterhouse and a nationally recognized authority on accounting and financial reporting for not-for-profit organizations. He was chairman of the AICPA Subcommittee on Nonprofit Organizations that wrote the 1978 landmark Statement of Position for Certain Nonprofit Organizations, and of the Accounting Advisory Committee to the Commission on Private Philanthropy and Public Needs. He was a member of the committee that wrote the second edition of *Standards of Accounting and Financial Reporting for Voluntary Health and Welfare Organizations,* and a co-author of the *Museum Accounting Handbook.* He served as an advisor to the Financial Accounting Standards Board in the early phases of its work on setting accounting standards for not-for-profit organizations, and to the New York State Charities Registration Office, as well as an adjunct professor of accounting at Lehigh University, his alma mater. After retirement from Price Waterhouse, he was president of a not-for-profit organization, the National Aeronautics Association. He now lives in the San Juan Islands off the state of Washington.

Richard F. Larkin is technical director of the Not-for-Profit Industry Services Group in the national office of Price Waterhouse. He is a certified public accountant with over twenty-five years of experience serving not-for-profit organizations as independent accountant, board member, treasurer, and consultant. He teaches, speaks, and writes extensively on not-for-profit industry matters and is active in many professional and industry organizations. He is a member of the Financial Accounting Standards Board Not-for-Profit Advisory Task Force, and chaired the AICPA Not-for-Profit Audit Guide Task Force. He participated in writing both the third and fourth editions of *Standards of Accounting and Financial Reporting for Voluntary Health and Welfare Organizations* and in the chapter on Not-for-Profit Organization in the seventh edition of the *Accountants' Handbook.* He graduated from Harvard College and has an MBA from Harvard Business School. He is currently a member of the AICPA Not-for-Profit Organizations Committee, and author of the chapter on not-for-profit organizations in the eighth edition of *Accountants' Handbook* by D.R. Carmichael,

Steven B. Lillian, and Martin Mellman, to be published this year by John Wiley & Sons, Inc.

Roger S. Bruttomesso is chairman of the Price Waterhouse LLP Not-for-Profit Industry Services Group and also serves as engagement partner on many of the firm's not-for-profit clients in the Metro New York region. He has over thirty years of experience serving the industry both professionally and as a volunteer. He is a past member of the AICPA Not-for-Profit Organizations Committee and is on the Board of the Nonprofit Coordinating Committee of New York City. He has spoken extensively on governance and accountability issues confronting not-for-profit organizations boards. He is a certified public accountant and a graduate of Dartmouth College, with an MBA from its Amos Tuck School of Business Administration.

John J. McNally is vice-chairman of the Not-for-Profit Industry Services Group and is located in the Washington, DC office of Price Waterhouse LLP. He has extensive experience in serving not-for-profit organizations as an auditor, consultant, and as a board member. He has represented Price Waterhouse in the business and not-for-profit communities for over thirty years. He currently serves as a member of a number of not-for-profit boards including the Hugh O'Brian Youth Foundation. He is also a member of the President's Advisory Board of LaSalle University, his alma mater. In 1995, he retired from the partnership of Price Waterhouse LLP.

Preface

This supplement further updates and expands the *Financial and Accounting Guide for Not-for-Profit Organizations* to include the latest developments in not-for-profit accounting and tax matters, as well as additional helpful reference material about various subjects.

Some of the more significant additions include:

- A new chapter revealing the truth regarding twenty-five common myths about not-for-profit financial management.
- A new chapter on internal accounting control, which provides guidance to directors and managers on such areas as the elements and framework of an internal accounting control system, and describes the specific controls applicable to not-for-profit organizations.
- A new chapter that examines the accounting issues related to fundraising.
- Discussion of the definition of a not-for-profit organization, and when certain organizations which are not-for-profit nevertheless must follow certain accounting principles applicable to for-profit organizations.
- Guidance on appropriate disclosures in cash basis financial statements.
- Summary of the provisions of the FASB Statement of Financial Accounting Standards, *Accounting for Certain Investments Held by Not-for-Profit Organizations.*
- Additional discussion of gifts which are passed through one not-for-profit organization to another.
- A step-by-step guide to preparation of a statement of cash flows.
- Summary of the provisions of the exposure draft of the AICPA Proposed Audit and Accounting Guide, *Not-for-Profit Organizations.*

The next supplement will include discussion of the final versions of the new AICPA audit and accounting guides for not-for-profit organizations and health care organizations, as well as other developments in these and other areas, many of which are well under way as this is written.

MALVERN J. GROSS, JR.
RICHARD F. LARKIN
ROGER BRUTTOMESSO
JOHN J. MCNALLY

Washington, DC
March 1996

Supplement Contents

Note to the Reader: Sections not in the main bound volume are indicated by a "(New)" after the title.

PART FIVE TAX AND COMPLIANCE REPORTING REQUIREMENTS

PART SIX SETTING UP AND KEEPING THE BOOKS

CHAPTER 1A (NEW)

Twenty-Five Myths About Not-for-Profit Financial Management

1A.1 ACCOUNTING PRINCIPLES

Myth 1: "Not-for-profit" accounting is very different from accounting used by for-profit organizations.

Fact: Most not-for-profit accounting is no different. The only area that is truly unique to not-for-profits is accounting for voluntary contributions received. Businesses make gifts, but they do not receive them. Accounting for gifts received, especially pledges, restricted gifts, and noncash gifts (gifts-in-kind) is sometimes complicated. See further discussion in Chapter 10.

Myth 2: Fund accounting is completely unlike anything in the for-profit world.

Fact: Every business except the extremely small business uses fund accounting. They just don't call it that. They call it accounting by department, subsidiary, division, branch, profit center, product line, operating unit, and so forth. But all of these sub-units of a business are exactly the same, from an accountant's viewpoint, as funds in a not-for-profit. Only the terminology differs. Also, businesses normally do not present information for multiple sub-units in their published financial statements; not-for-profits often present information for separate funds.

Myth 3: Depreciation of fixed assets is a tax loophole for businesses and has no relevance to not-for-profits.

Fact: Depreciation is a method of allocating the cost of long-lived assets over the accounting periods that benefit from their use. Failure to include this allocated expense in the reported expenses of a period understates the extent to which the organization has "used up" its available resources in carrying out its activities during the period. Excluding depreciation will make it seem as if the costs of various functions are lower than they really are; unwise decisions about allocations of resources may result. See further discussion in Chapter 7.

Myth 4: Recording a value for donated services of volunteers is a waste of time, as no cash is changing hands.

Fact: Volunteer time is a valuable resource to a not-for-profit. Failure to record the receipt of this resource understates the extent to which the organization has been the beneficiary of community support. Similarly, failure to record the corresponding expense understates the extent to which the organization has used available resources in carrying out its functions. Thus, unwise decisions about activities to be undertaken, and how they are to be financed, may result. Also, the organization may appear to outsiders to be less significant than it really is. See additional discussion in Chapter 10.

Myth 5: As long as we send some educational material along with our fund-raising appeals, the entire cost of the postage for mailing the appeal can be reported as program expense.

Fact: Reporting of any of the postage as program expense in this type of situation is possible only if certain specific criteria are met. The non-fund-raising portion of the material must have genuine educational value to the particular group of people to whom the appeal is sent; the content of the educational material must include a "call to action" on the part of the recipients; the audience targeted by the mailing cannot have been selected primarily for its giving potential. See further discussion in Section 14.8(c).

1A.2 FINANCIAL REPORTING

Myth 6: The more details of financial activities that are provided to the governing board and management, the better they will be able to manage the organization's affairs.

Fact: Many people on governing boards and in management are not as sophisticated about financial matters as people in similar positions in a business. People who achieve positions of leadership in not-for-profits are more likely to have done so because of technical expertise in the organization's program service fields or simply because they are highly motivated individuals interested in a particular cause. Although they may be very smart people, their training and experience often have not included much exposure to accounting and finance. Thus their ability and willingness to plow through large quantities of financial data to extract the information they need for decision making is limited. They are more likely to obtain a practical understanding of the real financial situation of an organization, or the financial effects of proposed decisions, if they have clear, *concise*, relevant, and credible data, instead of quantities of often largely irrelevant data. See additional discussion in Chapter 1.

Myth 7: Financial statements of not-for-profit organizations are always complicated and difficult for readers to understand.

Fact: If the statements are carefully prepared, with an emphasis on what is really important for the reader to know, the statements need not be confusing. See the discussion in Chapter 1 and throughout this book. Financial statements should pass the "non-accountant" test. See Section 1.2(a). If the statements fail the test, the recipients of the statements must complain, emphatically, to the preparer of the statements until understandable information is received. However, the reader is not excused from responsibility for making a reasonable effort to understand what is presented. Studying this book is one of the best ways for recipients to discharge that responsibility.

Myth 8: If the auditor's report does not refer to any departure from generally accepted accounting principles (GAAP), or contain any other unusual language, that means the financial statements are exactly correct in every detail.

Fact: An auditor renders an opinion, not a guarantee. What the auditor is saying is that the statements are not *significantly* misstated (do not contain material departures from GAAP), but the auditor could not possibly do enough audit testing to be able to guarantee that $5 (or $500 in a large organization) was not misclassified or missing somewhere. The presumption is that a person who relies on the information in the audited statements as a basis for making a decision about the organization will make the same decision as he or she would have made if the person had somehow had access to information that was completely accurate. See the discussion in Chapter 24.

Myth 9: "Profit" is a meaningless number for a not-for-profit.

Fact: Though not as important to a not-for-profit as to a business, the "excess of revenues over expenses" (the number in a not-for-profit's financial statements equivalent to profit of a business) does have significance to management and the governing board of the not-for-profit, and to other readers of the financial statements. For example:

- This number helps in assessing whether the organization is better or worse off financially at the end of the current year than it was the previous year.
- It tells whether the organization "lived within its means" during the year.
- A large negative amount (or continuing smaller negative amounts) can be an early warning sign of possible future financial problems.
- A large positive amount may be an indicator that the organization could be doing more to achieve its purpose.
- Comparison of the actual amount to the budgeted amount can indicate the extent to which management engaged in adequate advance planning, and the extent to which it actually managed the organization's affairs to achieve the planned goals.

1A.3 BUDGETS AND OPERATING RESERVES

Myth 10: A not-for-profit should never budget a deficit.

Fact: Although a budgeted deficit should not be undertaken lightly or regularly, it should not be dismissed out of hand. Circumstances in which it can be appropriate include:

- The organization has unrestricted net assets in an amount far in excess of needs foreseeable in the near future, and resource providers (members, donors, fee payers, etc.) are questioning the organization's need for additional funding.
- The organization is pursuing sources of funding that appear likely to come through, and expenditure of certain budgeted expense items can be made contingent on actual receipt of the funding (that is, if the funding is not received, these budgeted amounts will not be expended).
- An immediate need for the organization's services is so important (for example, relief for victims of a disaster) that the board is willing to commit to an activity even though funding is not presently in sight. There are adequate resources to survive in the short term, and the board makes realistic plans for quickly seeking the needed additional funding.
- A deficit can be budgeted in one program if resources to cover the deficit are available from surpluses in other programs, or from contributions or endowment income. The extent to which the costs of program services are to be subsidized from other sources is a major policy decision, which should be carefully considered by the board before a budget is approved.

See further discussion of budgeting in Chapter 20.

Myth 11: Because we lose money on every [patient we see in our clinic] [concertgoer who attends our concerts] [student who attends our college] [etc.], it isn't very important to closely monitor the amount we spend to provide our services. We'll just make up the difference from contributions.

Fact: When you plan to lose money in your program activities, it is *more* important to closely monitor costs so that you don't lose more than you planned. You originally limited the planned operating deficit to an amount that you believed could be covered by budgeted contributions and endowment income; if the deficit increases, there is no assurance that donors will be found to make up the additional amount.

Myth 12: No part of the principal of an endowment fund can ever be spent.

Fact: What most organizations call the "endowment" fund is really composed of three parts: true endowment, term endowment, and quasi-endowment. The true, or permanent donor-restricted, endowment can never be spent. The term, or temporary donor-restricted, endowment may be spent after the passage of a stated amount of time or the occurrence of a specified event. The quasi-endowment, or board-designated endowment, is legally unrestricted and can be spent at any time if the governing board votes to do so. See the discussion in Chapters 10, 13, and 15. Some organizations, which are fortunate enough to have accumulated fairly large unrestricted endowments, may feel uncomfortable admitting to donors (or faculty or orchestra members) that they have such large reserves. They believe that donors will be less likely to contribute (or faculty or orchestra members will demand higher pay) if the true financial picture is known. However, this is not justification for attempting to present a skewed financial picture. It is only fair to donors and others that they should have complete and fair financial information upon which to base their decisions.

Myth 13: Our board voted to restrict the unrestricted endowment, so we can't spend it.

Fact: A board cannot create a restriction when no *donor*-imposed restriction exists. A board can "designate" the unrestricted endowment; it can segregate the assets in a separate investment account; it can "appropriate" the assets for some future purpose (such as being held to produce investment income), but it cannot "restrict." Only an outside donor can cause the amount to be reported as restricted in the financial statements. Board-designated (the proper phrase) amounts must be reported as part of the unrestricted fund (or class of net assets).

The reason for this is that anything a board votes to do, it can later vote to undo; so the so-called board restriction is not really legally binding the way a donor-imposed restriction is. A donor-imposed restriction can be changed only by the donor, *if* the donor can be located *and* is willing to lift the restriction. (There is a legal procedure, known as *cy pres*, which can lift a restriction, but it is very cumbersome and will not be approved by a court except in very rare cases of extreme financial emergency.)

Myth 14: If we find ourselves with more unrestricted money than we have immediate uses for, or if we have a large restricted endowment, we can avoid having to explain to potential donors why we are so rich simply by moving all the excess assets into a separate "foundation" to be held for our benefit, so we don't have to show those assets on our balance sheet.

Fact: In this case, accounting rules will likely require that the financial data for the two organizations be combined for financial statement purposes, and readers will still see the entire amount of assets available for the benefit of the organization. See further discussion in Chapter 9.

Myth 15: The foundation is a separate legal entity, with its own tax-exempt status, a separate board, a separate office, and so on. If we don't actively control the other organization, surely we don't have to combine it.

Fact: Whether or not combination is required depends on the real nature of the relationship between the two organizations. Even if formal legal control does not exist, there may still be effective control through overlapping board membership or the parent having the power to appoint board members of the affiliate or to dictate how the affiliate uses its resources. Combination may still be required. Even if combination is not required, the two entities are considered related parties, and information about the existence of and transactions with the other organization is required to be included in each organization's financial statement footnotes. Thus, donors will still be aware of the other assets held for the benefit of the parent organization.

1A.4 FINANCIAL MANAGEMENT

Myth 16: Other board members can let the treasurer worry about the money.

Fact: Every board member has a fiduciary responsibility for all of the affairs of the organization, including finances. The treasurer may be charged with paying special attention to this area, but that does not excuse any board member from exercising diligent oversight in this and all areas. See additional discussion in Chapters 1, 21, and 23 of this book, and in *Tax Planning and Compliance for Tax-Exempt Organizations* § 5.5 by Jody Blazek (John Wiley & Sons 1993).

Myth 17: "Program" managers, such as the conductor of an orchestra, the nurse in charge of a clinic, the chair of a college history department, or the curator of a museum, can let the bookkeeper worry about the money.

Fact: See the response to the previous myth. Management decisions made by these persons can truly make or break an organization. Examples include decisions about which compositions an orchestra will perform, what hours to open the clinic, how many professors to hire in the department, and what kinds of objects to acquire for the collection. If these decisions are made without considering the financial consequences, the future of the organization will likely be jeopardized. Unfortunately, such people may not give adequate consideration to the financial implications of their operating decisions.

Myth 18: No one would ever steal from an organization that serves the needy, so internal accounting controls are not important to a not-for-profit.

Fact: Unfortunately, people do steal from organizations that serve the needy. If anything, internal controls are often more important to a not-for-profit than to a business. Although controls are sometimes looked upon by persons in the not-for-profit sector as nuisances that impede achievement of the organization's goals, reasonable controls will actually further that achievement. See the discussion in Chapter 23. Failure to establish and monitor adequate controls is a certain recipe for eventual organization failure. See also Section 23.1 of this supplement for examples of situations where weak controls almost destroyed (in one case, did destroy) not-for-profit organizations.

Myth 19: Because computers never make mistakes, if we keep our books on a computer, the resulting financial statements will always be completely accurate.

Fact: Information generated by a computerized accounting system is only as good as (1) the information that is put into the computer, and (2) the instructions by which the computer processes the data. Both are *very* much subject to human error, so computerized data should be scrutinized just as carefully as manual data to ensure that it is complete and accurate. See additional discussion in Chapter 34.

1A.5 GOVERNMENT REGULATION

Myth 20: Accountants for not-for-profits never have to worry about the Internal Revenue Service.

Fact: Some not-for-profits do have to compute and pay income taxes. These include those with unrelated business income, private foundations, not-for-profits that have a for-profit subsidiary, and not-for-profits that are not tax-exempt (there are some). Not-for-profits are also subject to most of the same requirements regarding payroll taxes as are businesses. In addition, organizations that have been granted "exempt" status by the IRS must always be careful to comply with the legal requirements for retaining that status. See further discussion in Chapter 26.

Myth 21: If the bookkeeper fails to pay the withheld payroll taxes over to the government, board members and other managers are protected from personal liability if the organization is a corporation.

Fact: The Internal Revenue Service can and will hold board members and managers personally liable for unpaid payroll taxes, regardless of a declaration of bankruptcy or the corporate form of organization.

Myth 22: If we would have to pay unrelated business income tax on the net income from a fund-raising activity, we shouldn't conduct the activity.

Fact: Having the net income after tax is better than having no income at all. Only if the organization receives a very large percentage of its total income from taxable activities will there be any concern about actually losing tax-exempt status. Filling out a tax return

(Form 990-T; see Chapter 27) is usually a small price to pay for a good source of income.

Myth 23: We don't have any assets or staff in [*state*], therefore we don't have to register before mailing our charitable solicitations to donors who live there.

Fact: Most states require even organizations that merely solicit by mail or media in the state to register before conducting the solicitation. See the discussion and list of states in Chapter 28.

1A.6 CONTRIBUTIONS

Myth 24: We should always accept every gift offered.

Fact: Some horses have bad teeth. For example, accepting a gift:

- that is restricted for a purpose not consistent with the organization's purposes will likely divert the organization's attention from what it had previously decided should be its priorities.
- for a compatible purpose, but with onerous limitations on exactly how the activity is to be conducted, can result in the recipient effectively ceding control of its operations to the donor. (A major university recently returned $20 million to a donor that had insisted on such limitations.)
- from a donor with a bad public image, with whom the organization would be embarrassed to be publicly identified, may hurt the organization's other fund-raising efforts. (Another university recently returned $500,000 to such a donor.)
- of a building, without adequate provision for paying the ongoing expenses of maintaining and operating the building, can expose an organization to considerable unbudgeted and unfunded liabilities.

- of land that is polluted or contaminated can make the organization liable for cleaning up the waste.
- annuity that requires the organization to pay out more than the value of the annuity is certainly not a good deal for the organization.

Myth 25: Getting an unrestricted gift is always better than getting the same amount as a restricted gift, because then we decide how to use the money.

Fact: Sometimes, but not always. For example, suppose your charity is a recipient of funding from a local federated fund-raising organization (such as United Way), which has a policy that if a member agency reports an unrestricted fund balance (net assets) amount in excess of one year's operating budget, the excess will be deducted from the next year's allocation by the federated fund-raiser. Further suppose that it is December 30th and you expect that your December 31 (your year end) unrestricted fund balance will be just about equal to one year's operating budget. Now suppose a major donor walks in the door and wants to make a large gift before year end (to get the personal tax deduction into the current year). Would you want the donor to make the gift unrestricted or restricted? If the gift is unrestricted, it will increase your year-end fund balance above the one-year limit, and the federated fund-raiser will deduct the amount from next year's allocation. Your donor has just effectively made a gift to the federated fund-raiser; you get no benefit from it. This illustrates the importance of open and frequent communication between accountants, management, fund-raisers, and donors. If one party (the fund-raiser, in this case) is not aware of all the consequences of various actions (soliciting unrestricted gifts), outcomes (the gift effectively ends up going to the federated fund-raiser) can be other than what is best for the organization (more resources available for its programs). Accountants and managers must take steps to ensure that such open communication occurs.

1A.7 A BONUS MYTH

Myth 26: There are no good books from which I can obtain an understanding of financial management for not-for-profit organizations.

Fact: You're reading one.

PART ONE

Key Financial Concepts

CHAPTER 2

Accounting Distinctions between Not-for-Profit and Commercial Organizations

2.2 PRINCIPAL AREAS OF ACCOUNTING DIFFERENCES

p. 13. *Add at end of section:*

(f) Other Areas of Difference (New)

Two other areas should be mentioned here: accounting for investments and functional reporting of expenses. Of the five areas discussed previously, only one—contributions—is truly unique to not-for-profit organizations; businesses do not receive gifts. Thus, there are no accounting principles addressing how businesses should account for contributions received. (Accounting for contributions made by for-profit organizations is covered in SFAS No. 116; see discussion in Chapter 10. The requirement is the reverse of the way the recipient accounts for the gift.)

The other four areas are not the subject of specific detailed accounting rules, except in certain aspects. As for those aspects, the requirements applicable to not-for-profit organizations are no different from the requirements applicable to for-profit organizations. The differences that exist in practice arise simply from the differing nature of the way not-for-profit organizations operate and the different concerns of readers of the financial statements of those organizations. In fact, practices followed by not-for-profit organizations are now very similar to those followed by for-profit organizations.

Definition of Not-for-Profit Organization

That leads to the question of just what is and is not considered a not-for-profit organization for purposes of deciding what accounting standards an organization is subject to. The new AICPA audit guide exposure draft discusses this issue in Chapter 1. It refers to a definition published earlier by FASB, which includes the criteria of receiving contributions, not having ownership interests, and having purposes other than making a profit. As to most organizations, it is immediately obvious whether they pass or fail this definition. Businesses fail it on all three counts. Most organizations that we think of as not-for-profit, such as colleges, orchestras, charities, churches, hospitals, and foundations, easily pass it.

Two types of organizations, which most people think of as being not-for-profit, do not clearly pass under this definition: clubs and associations. They do have purposes other than making a profit, and associations do not have ownership interests. However, many clubs do have ownership interests, and both types typically do not receive much in the way of contributions—they cover their costs from member dues and from sales of goods and services. (Note that "not-for-profit" and "tax-exempt" are not synonymous. Many organizations that are one are also the other, but there are exceptions in both directions.) Thus, the question arises as to whether clubs and associations should follow the accounting rules for not-for-profit organizations or the rules for for-profit organizations. The only two accounting areas in which there is really any formal difference are the two listed earlier: investments and functional expenses.

Accounting for Investments

With the issuance by the Financial Accounting Standards Board (FASB)—Chapter 19 discusses this organization—of formal accounting standards (SFAS No. 124) applicable to not-for-profit organizations for accounting for investments (see discussion of these standards in Chapter 8 of this supplement), there will be differing requirements for not-for-profit organizations and for-profit organizations in this area. Not-for-profits will follow this new standard; for-profits are subject to a different standard (Statement of Financial Accounting Standards (SFAS) No. 115, *Accounting for Certain Investments in Debt and Equity Securities*). Organizations that may operate as not-for-profit organizations but do not pass the preceding definition will have to follow SFAS No. 115, not the new standard.

Functional Reporting of Expenses

Accounting literature applicable to not-for-profit organizations has long required some degree of functional reporting of expenses (for example, see the discussion in Section 14.8(c)). Accounting literature applicable to businesses is largely silent on this subject, although in practice many businesses use a form of expense reporting that is partly functional. The new AICPA audit guide exposure draft (see Appendix D) also requires functional expense reporting for all not-for-profit organizations covered by the guide. Clubs and associations will have to decide on a case-by-case basis whether they believe they meet the definition of not-for-profit. Those that do not pass are not precluded from reporting expenses on a functional basis, and the authors encourage such reporting because they believe it is the most useful to readers of the statements.

CHAPTER 3

Cash versus Accrual Basis Accounting

3.1 CASH AND ACCRUAL STATEMENTS ILLUSTRATED

(a) Advantages of Cash Basis

p. 18. ***Add at end of subsection:***
For organizations that choose to present their financial statements on the cash basis, a question often arises as to what, if any, footnote and other disclosures should be made in the statements. Generally accepted accounting principles (GAAP; see page 420 in the main volume) require many different disclosures in accrual basis statements, but are mostly silent about the requirement to make such disclosures in cash basis statements.

The authors believe that, even in cash basis statements, certain disclosures should be made to fully inform readers of matters affecting the financial situation of the organization. These include information about, at least, the following (to the extent applicable to the organization) (After each item is shown the source, in GAAP, of the requirement.):

- Accounting policies and any changes in the policies used (APB Nos. 20, 22)
- Related parties (SFAS No. 57, SOP No. 94-3)

- Commitments, contingencies, and possible impairments of recorded assets (SFAS Nos. 5, 121)
- Extraordinary items, prior-period adjustments, and similar unusual matters (APB Nos. 9, 30)
- Major categories of fixed assets (if capitalized) (APB No. 12)
- Major categories, and fair market value, of investments (SFAS Nos. 107, 124)
- Mergers with other organizations (APB No. 16)
- Employee benefits (SFAS Nos. 87, 106, 112)
- Credit risk and information about financial derivatives (SFAS Nos. 105, 119)
- Restrictions on contributions and net assets (SFAS Nos. 116, 117)
- The format requirements of SFAS No. 117 (see discussion in Chapter 13)
- Joint costs of multipurpose activities (SOP No. 87-2 and its replacement)

CHAPTER 4

Fund Accounting and Internal Financial Reporting

p. 27. ***Add after third full paragraph:***

Fund accounting is also discussed in Chapter 16 of the new AICPA audit guide exposure draft (see Appendix D). The draft does not propose any significant new standards relating to fund accounting.

CHAPTER 6

Fixed Assets—Some Accounting Problems

p. 55. *Add at end of first paragraph:*
Chapter 9 of the new AICPA audit guide exposure draft (see Appendix D) also discusses accounting for fixed assets and depreciation.

6.2 ALTERNATIVES FOR HANDLING FIXED ASSETS

p. 60. *Change* **(b) Write-Off, Then Capitalize Method** *to* **(c) Write-Off, Then Capitalize Method.**

6.3 FIXED ASSETS WHERE TITLE MAY REVERT TO GRANTORS

p. 64. *Add at end of section:*
This method is discussed in the new AICPA audit guide exposure draft (see Appendix D). See also the discussion of gifts of the use of property in Section 10.2(d).

CHAPTER 8

Investment Income, Gains and Losses, and Endowment Funds

p. 83. ***Add at end of first paragraph:***
In November 1995, the Financial Accounting Standards Board issued a new statement of financial accounting standards, *Accounting for Certain Investments Held by Not-for-Profit Organizations.* A summary of its provisions appears in Appendix 8-A in this supplement.

8.1 ACCOUNTING PRINCIPLES

(g) Investments Carried at Cost

p. 88. ***Add at end of note 5:***
The FASB's guidance was issued as SFAS No. 124 in November 1995. See Appendix 8-A in this supplement. The requirement is that all marketable securities should be reported at current fair value, not at original cost or at lower of cost or market value. Nonmarketable investments, such as real estate, mortgages, oil and gas interests, and securities without a publicly quoted market value, should continue to be reported in accordance with whatever existing audit guide/Statement of Position the organization was previously following. Those methods are discussed in Chapters 14–17. This subject is also discussed in the new AICPA audit guide exposure draft (see Appendix D in this supplement).

(h) Presentation of Gains or Losses in the Financial Statements

p. 89. *Add at end of first paragraph of subsection:*
The new FASB statement on investments requires a new method of accounting for realized and unrealized losses on restricted endowment funds. It is summarized in Appendix 8-A (references to paragraphs 12–13) in this supplement.

p. 100. *Add at end of Chapter 8:*

APPENDIX 8-A

Accounting for Investments by Not-for-Profit Organizations

Summary of FASB Statement No. 124—November 1995

Effective date and transition:

Fiscal years beginning after December 15, 1995; early application encouraged (par. 17).

Option to apply either retroactively or prospectively (cumulative effect in current year)

—Usual APB No. 20 disclosures; effect on net assets reported for each class (par. 18–19).

Accounting for securities:

Coverage (par. 3):	—Equity securities (including options, warrants, rights) that have readily determinable fair values, except those accounted for on the equity method or investments in consolidated subsidiaries (par. 5). —Debt securities (not including derivatives).
Accounting principle:	All covered securities shall be reported at fair value in a balance sheet (par. 7). Use of cost, amortized cost, and lower of cost or market are prohibited. FASB specifically rejected the SFAS No. 115 three-category approach (par. 41–49).

Reporting investment gains/losses and income:

Investment gains/losses and income shall be reported in the statement of activities as changes in unrestricted net assets, unless their use is restricted by explicit donor-imposed stipulations or by law, in which case they are reported in the appropriate restricted class (par. 8–9). If a donor has explicitly restricted investment income from a fund, but is silent about gains, gains are considered to have the same restriction as income (par. 11).

Temporarily restricted gains and income whose restrictions are met in the same period as recognized may be reported as unrestricted, if the organization has a similar policy for temporarily restricted contributions (par. 10).

Reporting losses on investments of donor-restricted endowment funds:

In the absence of donor stipulations or law to the contrary:

—Losses shall reduce temporarily restricted net assets to the extent that donor-imposed restrictions on net appreciation of the fund have not been met before the loss occurs.

—Any remaining loss shall reduce unrestricted net assets (par. 12).

If losses reduce the assets of a donor-restricted endowment fund below the level required by donor stipulations or by law, gains that restore the fair value of the assets of the fund to the required level shall be classified as unrestricted (par. 13).

Examples:

Appendix C of the statement contains examples of the practical application of the standard as to reporting losses on restricted endowment funds.

Disclosures:

Composition of investment return (e.g., investment income, realized gains/losses on investments reported at other than fair value, net gains/losses on investments reported at fair value) (par. 14a).

Reconciliation of investment return to amounts reported in the statements of activities, if not all of the return is reported within an operating measure. Description of the policy used to determine the portion included in the measure of operations (pars. 14b, 100–106).

Aggregate carrying value by major types (e.g., equity, U.S. Treasuries, corporate debt, mortgage-backed, oil/gas, real estate) (par. 15a).

Basis for determining carrying value for securities other than those listed in par. 3 of this standard (par. 15b). (Carrying other investments at fair value is neither required nor precluded by this standard; par. 31).

Methods and significant assumptions used to estimate fair value of investments other than financial instruments if reported at fair value (SFAS No. 107 already requires this disclosure about financial instruments) (par. 15c).

Aggregate amount of deficiencies for all donor-restricted endowment funds for which the fair value of assets is less than the amount required by donor stipulations or by law (par. 15d).

SFAS No. 105-type disclosures about any concentration of market risk (par. 16).

SFAS Nos. 105, 107, and 119 disclosures about off-balance sheet risk, concentrations of credit risk, fair values of financial instruments, and derivatives, if applicable (par. 6).

Definitions (see Appendix E of the statement for complete definitions):

Debt security:	Any security representing a creditor relationship, including: redeemable preferred stock, convertible debt, a CMO required to be accounted for as a nonequity instrument, securitized debt instruments, strips. (Trade receivables and consumer and commercial loans are not securities, unless securitized.)
Equity security:	Any security representing an ownership interest in an enterprise, or the right to acquire or dispose of such interest at fixed or

determinable prices. (Does not include convertible debt or redeemable preferred stock.)

Fair value: The amount at which an asset could be bought or sold in a current transaction between willing parties. Quoted market price, if available.

Security: A share participation, or other interest in property or in an enterprise of the issuer, or an obligation of the issuer that (a) either is represented by an instrument issued in bearer or registered form, or, if not represented by an instrument, is registered in books maintained to record transfers by or on behalf of the issuer; (b) is of a type commonly dealt in on securities exchanges or markets; and (c) either is one of a class or series or by its terms is divisible into a class or series of shares, participations, interests, or obligations.

Practical application (not discussed as such in SFAS No. 124):

An organization that reports its balance sheet on a fund basis, and suffers a loss on investments of a donor-restricted endowment fund which reduces the fair value of the investments of that fund below the amount required to be maintained, will have to record an interfund receivable from the unrestricted fund to increase the value of the total assets of the restricted endowment fund to equal the required amount of fund balance. The entries are:

	Unrestricted fund	*Endowment fund*
Dr.	Loss	Due from unrestricted fund
Cr.	Due to endowment fund	Investments

Gains recognized in a later period which restore the assets of the endowment fund to its required level will also eliminate the interfund balance.

CHAPTER 9

Affiliated Organizations

9.2 DEFINITION OF THE REPORTING ENTITY

(a) Pass-Through Gifts

p. 105. *Add at end of subsection:*

Since the issuance of SFAS No. 116, this issue has become the subject of a great deal of discussion among not-for-profit organizations and the accounting profession. Many not-for-profit organizations which receive gifts that are at least partly passed through to other not-for-profits (these include federated fund-raisers such as United Ways, community foundations, and fund-raisers affiliated with universities and others) have expressed great concern about the effect that literal adoption of Paragraph 53 of SFAS No. 116 will have on the reported results of the organizations' fund-raising activities. Following is a more detailed discussion of this issue.

Thoughts on Donor-Designated Gifts

Background and existing accounting principle: Paragraph 53 of SFAS No. 116 states: "If a recipient receives cash that it must disburse to individuals identified by the resource provider or return the cash, neither the receipt nor the disbursement is a contribution for the agent, trustee, or intermediary."

The matter becomes important for organizations that receive gifts when the donor has explicitly or implicitly specified by name another not-for-profit organization which is ultimately to receive all or substantially all of the gift, or the income from the gift (referred to as *donor-designated gifts*). Such fund-raising organizations are often called *intermediary* organizations. A variation on this situation is the donor who specifies a field of interest, such as health, the arts, children, or a geographic area, for the use of a gift. Because the organization to which the donor directly makes the gift (the *reporting organization*) has discretion as to where to use such gifts within the field of interest or area, there is no question that the gift should be reported as revenue to the reporting organization.

Intermediary organizations come in three basic types:

1. Organizations that are controlled by, and which exist solely for the purpose of raising and/or holding money for, one or a small group of related organizations (sometimes referred to as the *parent organization*). Such groups are often named "The Friends of the [Museum]," "The [Hospital] Foundation," "The [Opera] Guild," "The [College] Alumni Association," or similar terms (and are sometimes called *captive fund-raisers*). Such organizations may be legally and operationally affiliated with the organization(s) they support. One can assume that by contributing to such an organization, a donor is implicitly stating an intention to support the parent organization.

   A variation on this type exists when the fund-raising organization, although established to raise money for one or a small group of related organizations (and often using the name of the supported organization) is legally, organizationally, and operationally independent of the organization(s) which it supports. The distinction lies in the degree of control exercised by the supported organization over the fund-raising organization. In practice, many different degrees of control are found, ranging from almost none to great. The facts and circumstances must be assessed in each case to decide whether there is sufficient control to consider the fund-raiser as merely an appendage of the supported organization.
2. So-called *federated fund-raising organizations,* which raise and/or hold money for many different organizations, usually in a particular geographic area. In some cases, the federated fund-raiser publishes

a list of organizations for which it is soliciting funds. The organizations for which money is raised are always legally and operationally independent of the fund-raiser. Despite the publishing of a list of supported organizations, gifts to federated organizations are presumed to be unrestricted unless the donor explicitly imposes a specific restriction as to use.

3. *Independent community-based organizations,* which exist wholly or partly to raise money for other organizations but are completely unrelated to any supported organization. They typically announce that one or a few named not-for-profit organizations will be beneficiaries of amounts raised, but they retain discretion to change the named beneficiaries in the future. These organizations act somewhat like grant-making foundations. Many clubs, so-called service organizations (e.g., Rotary), Junior Leagues, churches, and thrift shops perform this kind of fund-raising as part or all of their activities.

Federated fund-raisers come in three basic types:

- United Ways and similar community-based independent federated fund-raising organizations (including organizations that raise money for groups of organizations of a similar type, such as community arts funds, combined health appeals, Black United Funds, United Jewish Appeal, etc.).
- Combined Federal Campaigns (which operate within the federal government in a manner similar to United Ways and are often administered by the local United Way).
- Community foundations as defined by the Internal Revenue Service (Reg. § 1.170A-9(e)(11)).

There are two aspects to federated fund-raising which may result in less than the entire amount of donor-designated gifts raised being disbursed by the fund-raiser strictly in accordance with donors' instructions:

- Intermediary organizations generally take out a (usually small) portion of gifts, to cover their costs of fund-raising and administration, prior to remitting the balance to the designated recipients. The amount may be a fee, formally assessed as a stated percentage of the amounts raised or held (community foundations often do this), or may simply be the actual overhead expenses incurred for the year deducted from the total amount made available for allocation to all recipients (United Ways usually do this). Donors are presumed to understand that this occurs (although many, if asked, would in fact claim ignorance).

- Community foundations are required by the Internal Revenue Code to have, as part of the trust agreement establishing the foundation, a "variance power" giving them the right to redirect contributions as they see fit, regardless of donor designations. (United Ways also usually claim to have such power, de facto, as well, although it may not be explicitly stated.) Although this variance power is rarely exercised, it does exist. (This power to redirect gifts is *not* the same as the process of going to court—known as *cy pres*—to obtain legal permission to redirect the use of a donor-restricted gift when the original use of the gift has become impossible of fulfillment.)

Paragraph 53 (and all of SFAS No. 116) does not distinguish between captive, federated, and independent fund-raisers. It merely refers to "intermediaries." Whether the FASB considered the differences between the three types and deliberately chose not to make any distinction, or did not consider the differences, is not known at this time. The purpose of Paragraph 53, and of the more succinct statement in Paragraph 4 that SFAS No. 116 "does not apply to transfers of assets in which the reporting entity acts as an agent, trustee, or intermediary," is clearly to prohibit the reporting of revenue by an intermediary organization in two situations:

- When a not-for-profit organization establishes a controlled affiliate whose sole purpose is to raise funds for the organization, and to all appearances and for all practical purposes is an integral part of the organization; and
- When two or more organizations act together to inflate their income statements by passing gifts along a chain, with the intermediate members of the chain (which are often closely affiliated with other parties involved in the sequence of transfers) having only an

insignificant role in the process of passing gifts from the original donor to the ultimate charitable beneficiary(ies).

The percentage of total amounts raised by federated fund-raising organizations represented by donor-designated gifts varies from small to almost all for some organizations. United Ways' and community foundations' percentages are usually less than 50 percent, although at least one large United Way's percentage is 70 percent. In contrast, many combined federal campaigns receive almost all of their gifts with donor designations.

There is an additional dimension to this subject found mostly with community foundations: the distinction between the corpus of, and the income earned on, donor-restricted endowments. A donor may give the corpus of an endowment fund to the foundation with two stipulations:

- that the corpus must remain intact as a permanent endowment, and
- [the donor requests (although legally the donor cannot absolutely require)] that the income earned by the fund be given in perpetuity to a named not-for-profit organization.

A variation on this arrangement arises when a charity turns its endowment fund over to a community foundation, or a controlled affiliate, to manage and remit the income to the charity. Although the community foundation is the legal owner of the assets involved, it gains no economic benefit from either the corpus or the income of the fund, except for the management fee which it assesses against the fund each year. As to the corpus, the foundation acts solely as a trustee; as to the income, the foundation is in much the same position as a United Way that receives a donor-designated gift. Community foundations perform such functions as a service to donors and to the not-for-profit community in their area.

There is no real question about the applicability of Paragraph 53 to "captive" fund-raisers when the captive is controlled by either the parent or major donors. Even if the strict criteria for consolidation in SOP 94-3 (which if met, require consolidation, making the question of whether an intermediary should record revenue moot, although the fund-raiser may still issue its separate statements) are not met, most parents exercise enough control over a captive fund-raiser that it would clearly be inappropriate for the captive fund-raiser to record as revenue amounts it raises on behalf of its parent. Also, when a community foundation acts as trustee of another organization's endowment at the request of the organization, the beneficial ownership of the assets of the endowment lies with the other organization and is included on that organization's balance sheet. The community foundation is merely an agent of the organization and would show such amounts as assets and as amounts held on behalf of others.

The degree of control must, of course, be assessed in each case. If little or no control exists, then the intermediary is essentially an independent fund-raiser for purposes of this issue.

Current issue: Paragraph 53 has become a significant issue for federated and independent fund-raising organizations. A literal reading of Paragraph 53 has led some to the conclusion that even federated and independent fund-raisers should not report as revenue or expense any amounts which a donor has designated as being intended for another specific organization.

For organizations that receive a significant portion of their gifts from donors who have explicitly or implicitly designated the gifts for other not-for-profit organizations, the effect on the intermediary's statement of revenue and expenses of not reporting designated amounts as revenue (and expense) would be to seriously understate the actual amounts raised and distributed to beneficiaries. In the extreme case of 100 percent donor designations of gifts to the reporting organization, no revenue or expense would be reported at all (except the amounts retained by the intermediary to cover its overhead costs)!

The authors believe this would be an undesirable result. For organizations whose stated charitable purpose is to raise money for other organizations, which do not control and are not controlled by the reporting organization, it makes more sense for their financial statements to clearly report as revenue and expense the gross amounts raised and distributed to other organizations. That is what will tell readers of the statements the full story of the reporting organization's financial activities for the year.

In December 1995, the FASB issued an exposure draft of a proposed interpretation of SFAS No. 116.

Pass-Through Gifts—FASB Exposure Draft of an Interpretation of SFAS No. 116

Title: *Transfer of Assets in Which a Not-for-Profit Organization Acts as an Agent, Trustee, or Intermediary*

Interprets: Paragraphs 4 and 52-54 of SFAS 116, *Accounting for Contributions Received and Contributions Made*

Issued: 29 December 1995

Proposed effective date: Upon issuance (Expected to be May 1996)

Of interest to: All organizations that receive amounts which pass through one charitable organization to another charitable organization, and individuals involved with such organizations as auditor, accountant, manager, fundraiser, volunteer, donor, or other capacity.

Background: While par. 4 of SFAS 116 excludes transactions described in the title of the proposed interpretation, it gives little guidance about how to distinguish such transactions in practice. Also, since the issuance of SFAS No. 116, questions have arisen as to how par. 4 would be applied to gifts explicitly or implicitly designated by the original donor for a particular recipient organization. These questions have arisen especially from United Ways (and similar federated fund-raising organizations), community foundations, and fund-raising organizations that exist to support a single organization such as a college, hospital, orchestra, or museum.

After discussion with interested parties, FASB agreed to consider a clarification of SFAS No. 116 to provide more specific guidance for the practical application of these paragraphs of the statement.

Proposed interpretation: An organization that acts as an agent, trustee, or intermediary in the handling of gifts intended by the original donor to be passed through to another organization does not report contributions for such asset transfers (par. 3).

The term *intermediary* is used to describe an organization that acts solely as a facilitator of the process of making a gift between two other parties, but is not an agent of either party, a trustee, donor, or donee of the gift. For purposes of this interpretation, FASB intends the term to have this very narrow definition, not its general definition (par. 4). (Also see example in par. 180 of SFAS No. 116.)

The term *agent* refers to an entity that acts on behalf of one or more other entities (or individuals). FASB's definition covers organizations that (par. 5):

- (Agent for resource provider) Receive assets from a resource provider and agree to remit the assets, income from the assets, or both, to a specified beneficiary. If the resource provider's instructions cannot be complied with, the agent must return the assets to the resource provider or seek alternate instructions.
- (Agent for beneficiary) Agree to solicit assets from potential resource providers and remit the assets to the beneficiary; or the beneficiary can compel the agent to make distributions to it or on its behalf.

The term *trustee* describes an entity under a duty to hold and manage assets for the benefit of a specified beneficiary under a trust agreement. A trustee can be compelled to act in accordance with that agreement (par. 6).

In many cases it is not obvious in which capacity an organization is acting—as (1) agent or trustee, or (2) as a donee/donor. In case of ambiguity, an organization that receives assets is *presumed* to be acting as an agent or trustee in the following situations (par. 7):

- The organization is directed by the resource provider to distribute the assets to a specified third-party beneficiary and the *resource provider does not explicitly grant* the recipient organization the unilateral power ("variance power") to redirect the use of the assets away from the specified beneficiary (pars. 18, 23).

- The organization exists solely to raise, hold, or invest assets for another organization.
- The organization is directed by a resource provider to invest transferred assets in perpetuity and to return the income from the assets to the resource provider or its affiliate. (Also see par. 27.) This occurs when an organization turns over its endowment to another not-for-profit organization (typically a community foundation) to manage on its behalf.

If the pass-through organization has discretion sufficient to allow it to choose how the assets will be used, including choosing the beneficiary, then it is not an agent and may recognize a contribution (pars. 17, 21–22).

- If the resource provider merely specifies a field of interest, but leaves to the pass-through entity the selection of specific beneficiaries within that field, the pass-through entity has discretion and may recognize a contribution.
- If the only discretion available to the pass-through entity is the choice of the timing or amount of an individual distribution, or the choice of a department or purpose within the beneficiary organization, that is not sufficient to permit the pass-through entity to recognize a contribution (par. 26).

Receipt of assets as an agent, trustee, or intermediary would be accounted for as a debit to the asset and a credit to a liability account. Subsequent remittances of the assets to the intended beneficiary would be a debit to the liability, and the receipt and the remittance would not be reported as revenue and expense in the statement of revenues and expenses of the pass-through entity. The balance of the liability would be reported on the balance sheet under a caption called "Amounts Held for Others," or some similar term (par. 24). This will include amounts held by organizations such as community foundations as permanent endowment, with the income going to an organization specified by the donor of the endowment. Such amounts may be quite significant for some foundations.

(Note also that under SFAS No. 116 the beneficiary's future income interest in the distributions from the endowment is an asset which it must record on its books; the value of this interest will normally equal the fair value of the assets held by the foundation.)

Organizations that are agents or trustees, but which wish to include information in their financial statements about the entire amount of resources solicited, managed, or distributed, may do so in several ways (par. 30):

- In a statement of cash flows prepared on the direct method;
- In the statement of activity, as long as amounts received as agent or trustee are not reported as revenue (draft illustrates 3 examples);
- In a footnote or supplemental schedule. For example, a note or schedule could present an analysis of activity in the liability account, Amounts Held for Others, or a schedule of amounts raised and distributed, including certain ratios—see the following.

Adoption: Retroactive or prospective. Usual APB 20 disclosures (pars. 8–9).

Other comments on proposed interpretation: All persons who are involved as an auditor or a volunteer with a not-for-profit organization which acts in a pass-through manner (see background material) should become familiar with this proposed interpretation, and should bring it to the attention of leaders of the organization.

If adopted as proposed, the principal effect on pass-through organizations will be to reduce (compared with present practice) the amount of revenue and program expenses reported in the statement of revenue and expenses. In some cases, such as organizations that exist solely to support a single beneficiary, or federated fund raisers that receive a high proportion of their "gifts" from donors who have designated a specific beneficiary of the gift, future reported revenue and program expense amounts may be very small. This will have the side effect of distorting two ratios often used to assess the effectiveness and efficiency of not-for-profits: the ratio of program expenses to total expenses, and of fund-raising expenses to contribution revenue. Organizations will want to consider how they can best report to the readers of their financial statements the results of their activities—see preceding note on par. 30.

Pass-through organizations which will qualify as agents under these rules and wish to report donor-designated gifts as revenue will, in most cases, have to provide a mechanism for donors to explicitly grant variance power to the pass-through entity. This can be done on a standard form completed by donors.

(b) Combined Financial Statements

p. 107. ***Add at end of subsection:***
In October 1995, the FASB issued an exposure draft of a proposed statement of financial accounting standards on this subject. A summary of the proposal follows.

FASB Exposure Draft on Consolidations—October 1995: Summary of Principal Provisions Relevant to Not-for-Profits

Issued: 16 October 1995

Comment deadline: 15 January 1996 (Public hearing: 20–21 February 1996)

Effective date: Fiscal years beginning after 15 December 1996 (par. 37)
Early application encouraged
Comparative financial statements shall be restated (certain exceptions)

Supersedes: ARB 51, SFAS 94. (Amends various other statements.)

Scope: Applies to all entities that control other entities, regardless of the form of organizations involved (par. 4). (Exception: entities that carry substantially all assets at fair value, e.g., pension plans, mutual funds.)

Policy: A controlling entity shall consolidate all entities that it controls; unless control is temporary at the time that the entity becomes a subsidiary (par. 9).

Control: Control of an entity is power over its assets—power to use or direct the use of the individual assets of another entity in essentially the same ways as the controlling entity can use its own assets (par. 10).

Ways to control another entity's assets are having the power to:

- establish the policies of the controlled entity, as well as its operating and capital budgets;
- select, compensate, and terminate personnel responsible for implementing its policies and decisions.

Control is exclusionary (an entity may be controlled by only one entity at a time), regardless of whether that control is delegated or is not exercised.

The presence of legal restrictions that limit the freedom of discretion in the exercise of control does not overcome the existence of control itself. Such restrictions include those imposed by law, regulation, and contract. An example of the latter is a donor-imposed restriction on net assets of a not-for-profit entity. A controlling entity can cause the assets of the controlled entity to be used to remove certain restrictions, such as by paying off debt or paying penalties resulting from breach of contract, and fulfilling donor-imposed stipulations (if possible to be fulfilled) (par. 12).

Control can be achieved in two ways: legal control or effective control (par. 13).

- Legal control is normally achieved by having power to select a majority of a governing body (governing board, or partnership interest); voting stock ownership is the most common example.
- Effective control is control other than legal control.

Assessing the existence of control (pars. 14, 15, App. B): If by legal means, existence is usually apparent.

If by other means, careful consideration of relevant facts and circumstances is required. Absent evidence to the contrary, effective control shall be presumed if any of the following exist:

- Large minority voting interest (approximately 40 percent) and no other party or organized group has a significant interest;
- Ability, demonstrated by a recent election, to dominate the process of governing board selection;
- Unilateral ability to obtain majority voting interest by converting securities into voting securities;
- A relationship with an entity that: it (the reporting entity) has established, that has no voting rights, and that has provisions in its governing documents that (1) cannot be changed by entities other than the creator, and (2) limit the entity to activities that the creating entity can schedule to provide substantially all future net cash inflows or other future economic benefits to its creator (see also par. 154). (Gives example of University Foundation—par. 190.);
- Unilateral ability to dissolve the entity and assume control of its assets;
- Being the sole general partner in a limited partnership.

Other indicators, though not determinative, should be considered in each case (par. 158):

- Ability to cast a majority of votes in elections of directors;
- Ability to control the nomination and voting process for directors;
- Ability to appoint directors to fill temporary vacancies;
- Right to a majority of the net assets in the event of liquidation or other distribution;
- Being the sole creator of the other entity;
- A relationship that requires the two entities to work together for their purposes, for example, an organization is formed for the primary purpose of:

—holding and investing assets to generate income for another entity;

—holding assets to pay the debts of another entity;

—raising contributions for a specific charitable organization.

Examples of relationships that generally are *not* indicative of control (pars. 161–172):

- Manager and managed entity;
- Trustees, trusts, and beneficiaries (see also par. 150). (Note that a beneficiary's irrevocable interest in a trust is an asset of the beneficiary, but it does not give the beneficiary control of the assets of the trust itself.) (Gives example of third-party charitable trust—par. 206.)
- Grant-making foundations and their sponsors (e.g., corporate foundation);
- Federations, membership organizations, other associations, and their members, including associations of religious organizations (dioceses, synods, etc.);

Presentation of noncontrolling interests (pars. 22–24):

- Aggregate amount of noncontrolling interests is shown as separate component of equity.

  —Amounts attributable to the three net asset classes shall not be shown separately on the face of the statement.
- Share of consolidated net income is reported on face of statement of activity. (No specific format is required for not-for-profits—see par. 107.)
- Discussion of acquisition and disposition of a subsidiary (pars. 26–30).
- Parent and subsidiaries shall normally use the same accounting principles and the same fiscal period (rare exceptions) (pars. 31–33).

- Discussion of appropriateness of combined financial statements (pars. 34–35).
- Consolidated statements are primarily for the benefit of donors and other resource providers of the parent (par. 53).
- No need for different standards for businesses and not-for-profits (par. 55).
- Distinction between the objectives of businesses and of not-for-profits is not necessary in establishing conditions for consolidation (par. 79).

CHAPTER 10

Contributions, Pledges, and Noncash Contributions

p. 116. ***Add after carryover paragraph:***
Contributions are discussed extensively in Chapters 5 and 6 of the new AICPA audit guide exposure draft (see Appendix D).

10.1 EXPENDABLE CURRENT SUPPORT

(c) Investment Securities

p. 124. ***Add at end of subsection:***
See Chapter 8, and especially the new material in this supplement, for discussion of reporting investments in the financial statements.

10.2 GIFTS-IN-KIND

p. 129. *Add after end of section:*

(e) Services Provided by Other Organizations (New)

Some not-for-profit organizations are the beneficiaries of services provided at no cost by other organizations, often organizations with which the reporting organization is affiliated in some way. An example is a corporate foundation that occupies office space belonging to the company, uses office equipment belonging to the company, and has its functions performed by personnel on the company payroll, for which no charge is made by the company to the foundation. In separate financial statements of the foundation, the value of the "free" services should be reported as both a contribution and an expense. The expense would be reported in the categories appropriate to the nature and purpose of the services provided.

10.3 SUPPORT NOT CURRENTLY EXPENDABLE

(b) Pledges (Promises to Give)

p. 134. *Add after first full paragraph:*
SFAS No. 116 and other existing accounting literature are silent about how to present the allowance in the financial statements. There is no question about the presentation in the balance sheet: it is an offset to the receivable amount. Thus, if the organization has outstanding pledges totalling $75,000, and it estimates that 10 percent of that amount will be uncollectible, the allowance of $7,500 is deducted from the $75,000 and the net amount of $67,500 is shown.

What is not clear is how to present the reduction in the amount recorded in the statement of income and expenses to reflect the fact that not all of the recorded revenue will actually ever become available to the organization. One obvious possibility is to reduce the reported revenue amount by the uncollectible percentage. Another is to report the full amount of the pledges as revenue and the uncollectible amount as an expense. Because expenses are deducted from revenue, either method of reporting results in the same net excess of revenue over expenses for the year.

The exposure draft of the new AICPA audit guide (see Appendix D) proposes that the second (expense) method should be used. The authors disagree, and hope that the final guide will include the deduction-from-revenue method, as they believe that that method better reflects the reality of the way not-for-profit organizations manage pledges.

(d) Split-Interest Gifts

p. 139. ***Add at end of subsection:***
This subject is extensively discussed in Chapter 6 of the new AICPA audit guide exposure draft. The summary of that draft, in Appendix D of this supplement, lists the principal proposed requirements. This represents the first time that any accounting literature has included a comprehensive discussion of split-interest gifts, a most welcome development.

One proposed requirement that will have a significant effect on some organizations will apply in this situation:

> A donor establishes an irrevocable trust for the benefit of a named charitable beneficiary. The trustee is a third party (a bank, community foundation, or other trustee). The donor stipulates that all income earned by the trust is to be paid each year to the charity, but the principal of the trust must remain in perpetuity in the trust. Present practice is for the charity to record the amount received from the trust as income each year as it is received; the charity never records an amount representing its beneficial interest in the principal of the trust because it will never receive that entire amount for its use.
>
> The draft audit guide treats the charity's interest in the trust as a pledge—that is, an unconditional promise to pay annually to the charity an amount equal to the annual income earned by the trust—forever. SFAS No. 116 requires that an unconditional pledge be recorded by the recipient in full when the pledge is made. In this case the pledge is effectively made when the irrevocable trust is established, so at that time the charity must record the discounted present value (see the discussion on page 132 of the main volume) of a perpetual stream of payments of amounts equal to that annual income. The present value of such a stream of payments can usually best be measured by the current fair value of the assets of the trust.
>
> Thus, assume that a trust has assets worth $1 million, earning 5 percent ($50,000) per year. Under the old practice, the charity records revenue of $50,000 each year, forever. Under the new proposed rule, the charity would record $1 million as revenue (in the permanently restricted class) in the year

the trust is established. The charity would also record, as investment income, the $50,000 it receives each year. This will have the effect of making the charity look better off financially than it did in the past. Fund-raisers must be prepared to respond to donors' concerns over this apparent wealth. Recording the trust in this way is appropriate, however, because the arrangement is essentially equivalent to a gift directly to the charity of $1 million of permanent endowment. In both cases the charity will receive $50,000 of spendable income forever, but has no ability to use the principal of the gift.

CHAPTER 10A (NEW)

Accounting Issues Relating to Fundraising*

Accounting is important to fundraising for a variety of reasons. First, the results of fundraising—gifts—are reported in donees' (and sometimes in donors') financial reports. Second, those reports are used by many donors to help decide on whether and how much to give, as well as by regulators and evaluation agencies to assess the performance of donees. Third, federal tax rules restrict (to some extent) what donors and donees can do.

Donors as well as donees should always be aware of the accounting, reporting, and tax rules affecting their activities. Donees will raise more money if they consider donors' concerns. Donors will have their gifts used more effectively if they structure the gifts with donees' constraints in mind. Both groups will more greatly benefit society if tax rules are observed.

* Reprinted with permission from "Accounting Issues Relating to Fundraising." In J.M. Greenfield (ed.), *Financial Practices for Effective Fundraising* No. 3, Spring 1994. © 1994 by Jossey-Bass Inc., Publishers.

10A.1 ACCOUNTING FOR GIFTS

The accounting issues related to gifts are whether to record certain types, when to record the asset and the revenue, how to record gifts, how to show them in the financial statements. These issues are discussed here under the topics of pledges, revenue, restricted gifts, split-interest gifts, noncash gifts, donor tax deductions, pass-through gifts, and donor accounting. Relevant tax rules are noted.

In fall 1993, the Financial Accounting Standards Board (FASB) issued new accounting standards for gifts and certain other matters related to not-for-profit entities (Financial Accounting Standards Board, 1993a, 1993b). These new standards will take effect in 1995.

(a) Pledges

A pledge is a promise to give in the future. The pledge may be unconditional (that is, dependent only on the passage of time to become due) or conditional (that is, dependent on some future event or events, other than the passage of time, to become binding on the donor). Examples of conditions are raising of a specified "matching" amount, occurrence of a natural disaster such as an earthquake, and approval by a regulatory agency for a donee to proceed with some program activity.

By current accounting rules, conditional pledges are not recorded by the donor or donee until the condition is met. Footnote disclosure of such pledges is sometimes made. Unconditional pledges are recorded as assets when evidence of a binding promise is given the donee, except that colleges generally do not record pledges until paid. The assets are recorded at their estimated realizable value, which is net of an allowance for uncollectible pledges. The amount of the allowance is normally based on historical experience. The accounting literature does not specify whether pledges payable over a long period should be discounted to reflect the time value of money. In practice this is not done.

The new FASB standards require colleges to record unconditional pledges when made and require discounting to present value, with accretion of the discount being recorded as contributions income. Otherwise, there are no changes from existing standards for donees for recording the pledge asset.

As for donors, standards presently vary. Some foundations accrue grants payable; some do not. Other charitable donors generally accrue allocations and awards. For-profit donors sometimes accrue unpaid pledges, but not always. The new standards require all donors to accrue unconditional pledges payable as liabilities at their present value—the same rule as for donees, except applied backwards. The recording of the donee's revenue (expense to donors) is discussed below.

There are two related judgments that must be made in deciding whether or when to record a pledge: Is there really a pledge at all (versus a vague intention to give)? If so, are there any conditions to be fulfilled before the pledge becomes binding on the donor? These judgments must be made on a case-by-case basis; there are no formal rules. Some of the factors that should be considered in determining whether a pledge exists include whether the pledge is explicitly binding, whether the donee has announced the pledge publicly and the donor has not disagreed, whether partial payment has been made, the language used in the pledge document, whether the donee has made commitments based on reliance on the pledge, and how specific the pledge is in terms of amount, payment schedule, or use of the gift. As for conditionality, one should consider the exact language of the pledge, how explicitly the condition is defined, the likelihood of the event occurring and within what time period, and the extent to which occurrence can be facilitated by action of the donee.

Because recording (or not recording) pledges can make a considerable difference in the apparent financial condition of the donee (and maybe the donor), fund raisers will find that sometimes management will very much want (or not want) to record some pledges. Especially with major fund drives and with very large single pledges, as soon as plans are made or evidence of the pledge becomes apparent, the fund raiser is well advised to discuss with management of the donee, and with the donor, whether either has concerns about the way the pledge is to be accounted for. The fund raiser should be familiar with the different methods of accounting and the factors used in deciding which method is proper so that all alternatives can be discussed. For example, maybe both the donor and donee do not wish to record the pledge until a later period. In that case, if both agree, the language of the pledge can be written to make the pledge nonbinding or to include a condition that will not be met until the later period. Of course, there will be times in any fund raiser's career when one party wants to record the pledge and the other does not. Since the rules are the same for both, one of them will have to be flexible; maybe some inducement by one will convince the other. The fund raiser may be able to close the deal by facilitating such negotiation.

Bequests are special kinds of pledges in that they are often not made known to the donee until long after they are "made" (that is, written into a will). In general, bequests should not be recorded until the will has been probated and the court has given the executor authority to distribute the estate, because of the uncertainty as to whether there will be enough assets remaining after taxes, debts, expenses, and claims of other heirs to pay the bequest. (If the bequest is a specific one of modest size from a much larger estate and it appears very likely that the amount will be received, it would be appropriate to record this when the donor dies.)

(b) Revenue and Restricted Gifts

Even more important than when pledges are recorded as assets is when all gifts, including pledges, are recorded as revenue. This is because readers of financial statements usually pay more attention to the relationships among revenues, expenses, and fund balance (net assets) than they do to noncash assets.

The question of when revenue should be recorded is challenging. Presently, at least four different methods are used for different kinds of gifts to different kinds of donees. The determining factors are the type of organization, whether the gift is explicitly restricted by the donor, what kind of restriction exists, and whether the gift is in the form of a pledge. Briefly, the accounting literature specifies that explicitly time-restricted gifts ("for your 199X program") are revenue in the specified period; pledges are revenue in the period specified for payment (or if none is specified, then when paid); gifts restricted for a particular operating purpose ("for cancer research") are revenue: to a charity when received, to a college or a health care provider when the specific gift is spent, and to all other types of not-for-profits (those covered by the AICPA's Statement of Position 78–10) when any money is spent in meeting the restriction; unrestricted and endowment gifts are revenue when received. Practices relating to split-interest (deferred) gifts are complex and varied and are discussed later.

The new standard is that all unconditional gifts (including pledges) will be revenue when the gift or pledge is first received; a prepayment of a conditional pledge is still revenue only when the condition is met. The effect of this new standard will be that many not-for-profits will record some of their revenue sooner than they do now. This means usually higher revenue, larger excess of revenue over expenses, and larger fund balances. These organizations will appear to be in better financial condition than heretofore and thus will sometimes present fund raisers with the additional challenge of convincing prospective donors that new gifts are truly needed. Fund raisers will need to be adept at pointing out to donors that parts of the resources of the donee are legally restricted and cannot be used for general operations.

Heretofore, not-for-profits have reported revenue and fund balances by funds: current unrestricted, current restricted, plant (fixed asset), endowment, and sometimes others. The new standards call for only three "classes": unrestricted, or resources with no donor-imposed restriction; temporarily restricted, or resources with a donor-imposed restriction that lapses with the passage of time or is fulfilled by action of the donee; and permanently restricted, or resources with a donor-imposed restriction that never lapses or is never fulfilled.

Included in the unrestricted class will be all board-designated funds (quasi-endowment, for special projects, or other purposes) and property, plant, and equipment purchased with unrestricted resources. The temporarily restricted class will comprise operating restricted funds, term endowments, annuity and life income (split-interest) funds, unspent gifts restricted for acquisition of fixed assets, and fixed assets donated or acquired with funds restricted for that purpose. Pledges payable in a future period are considered implicitly time-restricted until that period. In the permanently restricted class will be permanent endowment and revolving loan funds.

Fund raisers soliciting unrestricted gifts will call donors' attention to the financial data for the unrestricted class, and similarly for other types of gifts. A donee may have a large endowment or other restricted balance but still be genuinely in need of unrestricted gifts because the restricted resources are not available except for specific purposes. Fund raisers should not, however, attempt to gloss over quasi-endowment funds and mislead donors into believing that these cannot be spent. Quasi-endowments are legally unrestricted and thus can be spent at any time with approval of the board of the organization. Some boards may wish to pretend that they cannot use quasi endowments, but since that is not the case, there is a risk of losing credibility with donors.

The main conceptual issue involved with classifying revenue is that of determining whether there is truly a donor-imposed restriction on a gift. This, too, is often a matter of judgment and may call for an interpretation of the donor's intent by the donor or by an attorney. Some of the factors to be considered include the exact language used by the donor, whether refund of unspent amounts is called for, the presence of nonprogrammatic "compliance" requirements, and the donee's intent in soliciting the gift.

As with pledges, the fund raiser may be able to work with the donor to structure a gift so that accounting for it does not have adverse side effects for the donee. (In this case, the method of recording by the donee does not affect the accounting by the donor.) For example, a charity may receive support from a federated fundraising organization whose policy is to deduct any unrestricted surplus as of year's end from the following year's allocation. An unexpected unrestricted gift received just before year's end can result in a surplus; the gift in effect ends up being turned over to the other funder next year. However, if approached with a proposal to restrict the gift to some specific anticipated need of the donee, the donor may be willing to comply, thereby retaining the gift for the charity. Fund raisers must always be up-to-date on the entire fundraising and financial picture of an organization, and alert for opportunities to plan gifts to achieve maximum benefit for both parties.

Another accounting issue of concern to fund raisers is when and how program expenses paid with restricted gifts are reported and how these expenses are "matched" in the financial statements with that revenue. Current principles are that when restricted resources are available for a particular activity, and money is spent to conduct that activity, it is presumed that the restricted resources were used, even though the entity may also have unrestricted resources available and may even have specifically used money identified as unrestricted. In the latter case, the restricted resources that remain are then considered unrestricted, by virtue of the donor's restriction having been fulfilled. An exception to all of this is that colleges presently have the option of specifying whether the resources used were unrestricted or restricted. FASB's new standards specify that restricted resources are always deemed to have been used first, thus removing the present flexibility enjoyed by colleges to "hold back" restricted gifts for future use even while fulfilling the donors' restrictions with other money.

An additional aspect of reporting program expenses is where they are shown in the statement of revenue and expenses. Under existing practices, expenses financed with restricted resources are reported in the restricted fund. FASB's new requirement is to report all expenses in the unrestricted class, with restricted resources being reclassified (transferred) to the unrestricted class to match the expenses incurred. Fund raisers will now have to be prepared to explain to donors how the donee reports the use of their gifts: At first, it will look like no restricted gifts have been used. Since all expenses will be in the unrestricted class, the restricted class will show no expenses, which some donors will question. Also in computing the ratio of program expenses to contributions (an indicator used by some to evaluate a donee's performance), fund raisers will take the program expense number from the unrestricted class but have to add together unrestricted and restricted gifts to obtain the denominator of the ratio.

(c) Split-Interest Gifts

This category refers to the several types of gift arrangements involving "split" interests, that is, both the donor and the donee receive benefits, at least for a while. The task of accounting for the five stages in the life of a split-interest gift (initial receipt; periodic income; periodic payments to life tenant; periodic actuarial revaluation of remainder interest, if applicable; and final distribution of corpus) is not well defined in accounting literature. Further, accounting for different types of gifts varies with the exact gift arrangement, and sometimes with different types of organizations. Hence, a wide variety of methods is used in practice.

Space does not permit a full discussion of all of the accounting issues for these gifts, but fund raisers should be aware of which methods are used by an organization. If a type of gift not previously received by an organization appears in prospect, the fund raiser should discuss the proposed accounting with the organization's chief financial officer and, maybe, its independent auditor so that appropriate information can be communicated to the donor if requested. Further, because tax attributes of these gifts are complex, and significant to the donor, the fund raiser should be certain that donors are receiving adequate professional advice prior to making these gifts.

Briefly, the accounting issues are as follows: Is the initial receipt of the gift recorded as revenue, deferred revenue, or an addition to the fund balance? Is the initial amount discounted to present value? Are the annual income and the payments to the life tenant recorded as revenue and expense of the donee? How is any actuarial adjustment presented? And how is the final distribution presented in the donee's financial statements? The answers to these questions are relevant in determining how to assess the performance of the organization in soliciting and managing these gifts.

(d) Noncash Gifts and Donor Tax Deductions

This section discusses issues related to the recording of gifts that are not in the form of cash or marketable securities. These gifts include gifts of assets (real estate, equipment, supplies, collectibles, and nonmarketable investments), donated services of volunteers, and the use of property. The two questions here are, Should the gift be recorded at all and, if so, at what amount?

Generally, gifts of assets are recorded at their estimated fair value, which is theoretically the amount the donee would have had to pay on the open market to acquire items of similar utility. Fair value can be determined by an appraisal, reference to sellers' catalogues or price lists, recent purchase prices of similar items, or other sources. Items sold shortly after receipt are usually recorded at the selling price. (In certain circumstances, sale of an asset by the donee can affect the allowable tax deduction by the donor.) Certain assets are not always recorded: gifts of emergency supplies to disaster relief agencies, because of the logistical problems of counting, valuing, and tracking large quantities of diverse and difficult-to-value items such as used clothing under disaster conditions, and museum collection objects, because of the difficulty in determining meaningful values for many items, and the unique status of such objects (usually retained indefinitely and not directly income producing; see also the next section on pass-through gifts).

Fund raisers soliciting such gifts should be aware of what the donee's policies are about accounting for them, in case donors inquire. Sometimes the donor will ask what value the donee is placing on a gift. Usually the donor is looking for support for the tax deduction to be taken. While a donee may choose to satisfy a donor's pure curiosity, the donee should, under no circumstances, assume the role of an appraiser for the donor. In fact, for gifts valued over $5,000, the tax code forbids a donee from appraising such gifts. It is the donor's responsibility to obtain an independent appraisal for tax purposes. The donee does not wish to become involved in a possible later dispute between the donor and the Internal Revenue Service (IRS) over the proper value of the property.

For gifts over $500, the donor must complete IRS Form 8283 and attach it to the tax return. If the gift is over $5,000, the donee will be asked to sign the form; this signature merely acknowledges receipt of the items and in no way attests to their value. If the donor appears to misunderstand this, the donee should so inform the donor. Further, if the donor does not appear to be aware of the requirement to file Form 8283, the donee should advise the donor of this. Both of these pieces of advice will likely avoid later donor unhappiness, which, were it to occur, would certainly reduce the likelihood of future gifts. Finally, if the donee sells an item within two years of receipt, the donee must advise the IRS (and the donor), on Form 8282, of the amount received from the sale. Donees are well advised to warn donors of this requirement. The donee does not want a donor who overvalues the amount of a deduction to blame the donee for a personal tax audit that is triggered by a report of a later sale of the item for a much lower amount.

Accounting for donated services of volunteers and the use of property is another area of controversy Some accountants argue that no value should be recorded; some believe that it is appropriate to record such contributions. Arguments against recording usually focus on (1) the fact that there is (in most cases) no effect on the excess of revenues over expenses or on the fund balance because recording these items usually involves recording equal amounts of revenue and expenses (an exception is when the volunteers create a capitalizable asset such as a building), (2) the fact that no cash changes (or ever will change) hands, and (3) the alleged unnecessary effort required to track the hours worked by volunteers and assign a value to them. Arguments for recording are that the effort to track and value volunteers' hours is not that great and, mainly, that failure to record these contributions and related expense understates the extent to which the organization has been the beneficiary of public support, and the extent to which the organization has utilized available resources (including volunteers) in performing its activities. I concur with these latter points.

The accounting literature is not very definitive, and practice varies widely. There is an understandable, but not defensible, tendency to be more desirous of recording a value for volunteers who are performing program functions than for those working in administration or fundraising. In fact, fundraising volunteers are rarely recorded for two other reasons: Many of them often work more or less on their own and thus are not under the degree of supervision that allows easy tracking of time worked, and an objective determination of a value to assign per hour is usually not possible, due to the lack of comparable paid work. Another category of volunteer almost never recorded, for the same reasons, is the board member.

FASB's new requirements standardize accounting for volunteer services by means of two criteria that, if either is met, require recording; if neither criterion is met, recording would be barred. (Disclosure in a note added to the financial statements of unrecorded contributed services will be encouraged.) The two criteria are as follows: (1) if the services create or enhance nonfinancial assets and (2) if the services require specialized skills, are performed by persons possessing those skills, and would otherwise have to be purchased by the recipient if volunteers were not available. The definition of specialized skills remains to be worked out, and the determination of whether the organization would have otherwise paid someone to perform the services will require judgment in each situation. The services will be valued in the first case by the value of the asset (less any purchased components), and in the second case by the amount the provider did not charge (which such persons can easily state).

One nonaccounting question is often raised by volunteers: Can the volunteer take a personal tax deduction for the value of the time spent? The answer is unequivocally no, per Income Tax Regulation 1.170A-1(g). Volunteers can deduct certain out-of-pocket expenditures incidental to their work as volunteers.

Fund raisers should be aware that all of the rules defining amounts deductible by donors are complex, and donors should consult their own tax advisers for guidance. Fund raisers should not, unless they are professionally qualified in this area, give tax advice to donors. This has a high probability of leading to trouble later. Areas in which the rules are especially complicated, and fund raisers should warn donors to seek competent advice, include all noncash gifts, especially gifts of inventory by businesses, gifts of life insurance, and gifts of appreciated property; gifts to recipients that are classified as private foundations; gifts that constitute a significant percentage of the donor's income for the year; gifts that are bargain sales; gifts payable over several years; bequests; gifts of a partial interest in property (including the split-interest arrangements discussed earlier); and gifts for use outside the United States.

(e) Pass-Through Gifts

Several related accounting issues come into play whenever the simple donor-donee relationship is expanded to include one or more additional parties. The additional party could be a charitable entity whose purpose is to solicit gifts for another organization, or any organization that holds and manages assets for the benefit of an operating not-for-profit entity.

Some not-for-profits establish "captive" or controlled affiliates to either solicit gifts or hold assets; others participate in noncontrolled federated fundraising organizations such as United Way. Some donors give donations to independent third parties such as a bank trust department or a community foundation with instructions to invest the assets and pay the income to specified charitable beneficiaries. In many cases the trustee may not invade the principal of the gift, but in some cases the trustee has discretion about such invasion.

Whenever a not-for-profit establishes a controlled affiliate, a determination is required as to whether the affiliate should be combined with the "parent" for purposes of the parent's financial statements. A parallel determination is whether, in separate financial statements of the affiliate (if prepared), any gifts made to it are properly reported as its revenue or whether such gifts are merely amounts held on behalf of the parent, and not revenue of the affiliate. Such amounts held are reported on the balance sheet as liabilities.

These determinations depend on an assessment of how much control is exercised by the parent over the governance, management, and activities of the affiliate. If the control is very strong, the affiliate should be combined into the parent's financial statements, and in separate statements the affiliate should report gifts to it as amounts held, not as revenue. If control is very weak, the affiliate need not be combined, and gifts to it are reported as its revenue (and later reported as grant expense when remitted to the parent). A great deal of judgment is required to decide whether the level of control is high enough to qualify as strong. The accounting literature is not very well defined on this issue; practice is diverse (although in cases where a related party is not combined, disclosure of the existence of and nature of transactions with the related party is required). AICPA has issued an exposure draft of new standards (AICPA, 1993b), and FASB is also working on improving the usefulness of standards in this area.

Factors that should be considered in assessing the strength of control include the degree of overlap of governing boards and management; relevant provisions of governing documents, contractual or other agreements; the extent of required review and approval of the actions of one entity by the other; and the impression given to outsiders by the organizations' fundraising material and annual reports. The last factor is important: When a donor gives to the affiliate, does the donor think of it as really a gift to the parent? If so, there is likely strong control.

When assets functioning as endowment are held by an independent third party, the charitable beneficiary of the income normally does not include such assets on its balance sheet. If the trustee has discretion as to when and in what amounts to pay income to the charity, the charity records such amounts as contributions when received. If the trustee has no discretion but must pay over all income as received, the charity records this as investment income.

In both of the above situations, the charity's receipt of income from the third-party trustee distorts certain normal relationships among financial statement data. In one case, contributions, but not related fundraising expenses, are reported by the charity; in the other, investment income is reported, but the underlying assets are not shown. Thus, persons seeking to analyze financial data for organizations where certain activities are carried out by other entities must consider the impact of any of the accounting practices just described on the data being analyzed, as "expected" relationships will often not be observed. Specifically, fund raisers will find that evaluation of the fundraising efficiency for such organizations requires more than merely dividing reported fundraising expenses by reported contributions.

(f) Auditing and Internal Accounting Controls

These subjects, well covered in other literature, are mentioned briefly here to reinforce their importance. Primary responsibility for establishing sound controls and arranging for audits usually belongs to the organization's accounting staff, not the fund raiser. However, these matters are of concern to the fund raiser because of the close relationship among the functions of raising, controlling, and auditing gifts. If the fund raiser senses a lax attitude of management or the accounting staff about these matters, he or she is well advised to bring the problem to the attention of someone in the organization. Not only can weak controls lead to a loss of assets by the organization, but also publicity about instances of loss will hurt the fund raiser's ability to attract gifts.

Contributions to charities are inherently the most difficult of all types of accounting transactions over which to establish strong internal controls and a thorough audit process. This is due to the nonreciprocal nature of the transaction: Cash comes in but no goods or services are provided in exchange. Thus, many of the checks and balances used in businesses to control sales and cash receipts are not available to a charity. This means that while management personnel should try to establish as strong a control environment as possible, the challenge to do so is great, and they must always be alert to weaknesses that could allow misappropriation of assets.

10A.2 ACCOUNTING FOR FUNDRAISING EXPENSES

Reported fundraising expenses figure prominently in many assessments of the efficiency and effectiveness of fundraising efforts and of the charity overall. Whether this is really good or bad is left to others to discuss, although I believe that too much importance is often ascribed to fundraising expenses. Nevertheless, fund raisers must understand them to be able to discuss them intelligently.

Fundraising expenses are those expenses incurred to induce donors to contribute to an organization. Such expenses must be reported separately in the financial statements of organizations that solicit significant amounts of gifts from the general public. The new FASB standards will require such disclosure by all not-for-profits (except where these costs are immaterial to an entity). Issues relating to these expenses include what types of expenses should be called fundraising, when they should be reported as expenses, and when and how to allocate multiple-purpose expenses.

(a) Expenses That Are Fundraising

The short definition given above requires elaboration to fully describe all of the various types of activities comprehended. These include planning fundraising campaigns, managing the fundraising process, actual public solicitation costs (mail, media, and so on), applying for foundation and government grants, training and supervising fundraising volunteers, staff time required to participate in federated fundraising campaigns, and other costs intended to advance the solicitation effort.

Some costs are usually not charged to fundraising, such as accounting for contributions received, which is considered an administrative cost. Some consider the cost of recruitment of all volunteers to be a fundraising expense, others consider it an administrative expense (akin to hiring paid staff), and still others would have the cost follow the duties of the volunteers being recruited. The accounting literature does not speak to this point, and practice varies; so if such costs are significant, financial statement users should inquire as to which method is followed.

The subject of recording a value for the time of fundraising volunteers was mentioned earlier in the discussion of noncash gifts. Generally, as noted, such values are not recorded. Thus, comparison of fundraising efficiency between two charities, one of which relies heavily on volunteers for fundraising and the other of which uses paid staff, is not very meaningful (see also the earlier section on pass-through gifts for a discussion of fundraising cost issues related to such gifts).

One other category of costs related to fundraising is usually not reported as fundraising expense: costs directly benefiting participants in "special events" such as dinners, parties, games, athletic activities, and sales of items such as cookies and greeting cards. For example, at a dinner, costs of food, decorations, entertainment, and prizes are for items that benefit attendees, not the organization. On the other hand, costs of invitations, planning, and publicity do not directly benefit attendees. Costs benefiting attendees are reported as an offset to revenue from the event, other costs are fundraising. So if one pays $500 a plate to attend a dinner and the costs to the organization of putting it on are $65 for food and entertainment and $20 for publicity, the financial statements would show $500 of gross revenue less $65 direct costs for net revenue of $435, and fundraising expenses of $20.

Two tax matters should be noted here: If the attendee could have purchased a comparable dinner for, say, $100, the tax deduction available is $400 ($500 payment less $100 value received); and in the IRS Form 990 filed by the organization, it will report $400 of the ticket price as a contribution (line 1) and $100 as proceeds from special fundraising events (line 9a) The $65 is shown as an offset to the $100 (line 9b), and the $20 as fundraising expense (line 15). Fund raisers should have at least a basic understanding of these tax matters, especially those that affect donors' deductions. Further, the organization must advise donors who receive an item of significant value in return for a donation (dinner, books or records, and so on) of the portion of their payment that is not tax deductible; failure to do so (or the use of vague phrases such as "Your gift is deductible to the extent provided by law") can attract an IRS penalty.

(b) When to Report Fundraising Expenses

Although fundraising costs incurred in one period often result in contributions received in future periods, accountants generally require that these costs be expensed in the period incurred rather than partly deferred to future periods. This requirement is due largely to the inherent uncertainty of the response to any fundraising activity, which leads to an inability to accurately assess the extent to which such expenses actually have any remaining value at the end of the year in which they were incurred. Even expenses incurred in one year to develop long-range giving programs, such as capital campaigns or deferred (split-interest) gifts and bequests, must be reported as expenses when incurred, not deferred until gifts are received. (One exception to this rule is that unused supplies of printed materials can be carried as inventories, so long as they are reasonably expected to be used in future periods.) Thus, comparison of fundraising expenses reported in one accounting period with contributions reported in the same period may or may not accurately reflect the real cause-and-effect relationship of these items.

Currently, a project is under way at AICPA regarding accounting for advertising costs for businesses. In the past, such costs have also been expensed when incurred. AICPA is proposing to allow deferral of costs of soliciting so-called direct-response advertising (solicitation of mail or telephone orders) when a historical relationship can be demonstrated between such costs incurred in one period and sales in a subsequent period, which the nature of direct-response advertising makes possible. Although this advertising project explicitly excludes fundraising efforts of not-for-profits, the parallel with fundraising is so obvious that consideration may be given to extending the principle at some later date.

(c) Allocation of Expenses

The general question of allocation arises whenever an expense benefits more than one activity. For example if office space is shared by two departments, the monthly rent is allocated to the departments, usually on the basis of amount of space occupied. Similar allocations are often required for salaries, utilities, supplies, and other expenses. In most cases, the basis of allocation can be readily determined: salaries by time spent, supplies by usage, or occupancy by space occupied. The allocation process does require additional record keeping: time sheets or effort reports by personnel, estimates of supply usage, or computation of space occupied. Then work sheet calculations produce the allocated amounts.

Once total fundraising costs are determined, by adding directly charged and allocated amounts, it may be desired to subdivide these costs into components representing the costs of each separate fundraising activity, for example, various separate mailings, television advertisements, door-to-door, and solicitation of grants. The process is the same as before; however, the smaller the final pieces, the more difficult it becomes to be objective about the allocations, and the less precise the outcome. That is, in attempting to subdivide fundraising expenses, one must recognize that the result does not have the same level of accuracy as achieved with larger-scale amounts.

One particular allocation problem requires separate discussion: allocation of "joint" costs. These occur when a cost item simultaneously benefits more than one function and there is no objective method available to decide how much of the cost to allocate to each function. In fundraising, this situation most often occurs with multiple-purpose mailings, such as those containing both educational material (for example, the seven warning signs of cancer) and an appeal for donations. The printing costs of each component are not at issue here; those are charged directly to the respective function. The issue is the joint costs: the outside envelope, mailing list rental, staff time to coordinate the mailing, and (usually the largest item) postage.

Two questions must be answered: Is it at all appropriate to allocate the joint costs and, if so, on what basis? These questions may seem trivial, but they are not. If it were always true that such mailings had a bona fide educational purpose, then the question of whether to allocate would be moot. However, often such mailings are really just solicitations, and any educational component is an afterthought, added to take advantage of the mailing going out anyway. How does one distinguish the genuine program activity? State charity regulators are especially concerned about this issue.

The accounting profession has published guidance in AICPA (1987), *Accounting for Joint Costs of Informational Materials and Activities of Not-for-Profit Organizations That Include a Fund-Raising Appeal.* (AICPA [1993a] has produced a new statement that amplifies and clarifies but does not change the basic premises of the 1987 document.) This standard defines several requirements that must all be met in order to allocate joint costs to functions other than fundraising. These requirements are as follows: (1) there must be verifiable evidence of the reasons for conducting the activity, (2) the content of the activity must include a bona fide purpose other than fundraising, (3) the audience targeted must have a legitimate interest in the non-fundraising component of the activity, and (4) the non-fundraising component must include material designed to motivate its audience to action other than contributing to the organization.

Clearly, professional judgment is required in deciding whether these requirements are met. The first requirement is judged partly on the answers to the other three, as well as on criteria such as written management plans and board resolutions, and assignment of overall responsibility for the activity to persons other than fund raisers. The second requirement is judged on the inherent value of the material and its consistency with the stated purposes of the organization. The third requirement has two components: the assumed wealth of the audience (as measured by income statistics for the geographical areas targeted, under the assumption that a wealthier audience is more likely to have been targeted for its fundraising potential) and the presumed benefit to the audience of receiving the information (measured by data such as epidemiological statistics for a disease, demographic data, or other methods). The fourth requirement is best illustrated by an example. If the "educational" material merely described the seven warning signs of cancer, that would not count. It must say, "Here are the seven warning signs of cancer; if you notice any of them, *go* to your doctor." The action is "go to your doctor." The presumption is that learning about something is of real value only when one takes beneficial action based on that knowledge. The action called for must be fairly specific: "Don't pollute" is too vague, but "Don't dump used motor oil in a storm drain" would qualify. The action may benefit the person receiving the message, or it could also benefit other people ("Don't drink and drive") or the environment (the motor oil example).

When working with a charity to plan a fundraising activity that will include an educational component, fund raisers should be aware of these requirements so they can help the charity comply with the accounting rules if allocation of some of the costs to program activities is desired.

The second allocation question is what and how to allocate. What to allocate was discussed earlier; how is often a difficult question. It might seem that one could merely measure the relative quantities of educational versus fundraising material (lines of print, square units of space, or some comparable measure). However, first, not all material is of equal value: How does one count photographs, for example, or blank space used for emphasis of surrounding material, or various sizes of type, or sweepstakes tickets? Second, if relative quantity were the sole measure, charities attempting to minimize fundraising costs would simply use the technique well known to writers of school term papers: padding. Educational material would expand to fit the desired outcome, likely with little or no additional benefit to readers; in fact, the benefit might decrease as the message drowns in a sea of fluff. As a result, judgment is significant to the question of how to allocate. Certainly content can be considered, but so too the relative impact and usefulness of the material, the apparent intent of the activity, the need of the audience for the educational material, and other relevant factors.

(d) Assessing Fundraising Efficiency

Although this subject is not an accounting matter, it does depend partly on accounting data. What I have shown here is that the use of accounting data to help assess fundraising efficiency must be done carefully, due to the interaction of various accounting principles that determine when and how contributions and fundraising expenses are reported in financial statements.

10A.3 OTHER TAX CONSIDERATIONS

Besides the various tax matters discussed earlier in this chapter, one more is of concern to fund raisers: private foundation status. The subject does not come up often, but when it does, the consequences can be severe for both donor and donee. Thus, fund raisers should know enough to recognize a potential problem and seek professional advice.

Briefly, all organizations exempt from tax under Internal Revenue Code Section 501(c)(3) (the section that covers most entities to which tax-deductible gifts may be made) are either private foundations or public charities. Public charity status is much more desirable for both the charity and its donors, since private foundation status imposes a number of rather onerous constraints on the charity as well as limits the amount of tax deduction available to donors in some cases.

The determination of whether an organization is considered a private foundation is based to a great extent on from whom and in what amounts contributions are received. Thus, when soliciting gifts for a charity, fund raisers must be conscious of what types of gifts could include a risk of the charity being reclassified as a private foundation as a result of the gift. (Tax specialists use the word *tipping* to refer to this occurrence: The public charity is tipped into private foundation status.) Or, if the organization is already a private foundation, the fund raiser should be sure that prospective donors are aware of that fact and its consequences to them. (It is not within the scope of this chapter, or normally within the professional competence of the fund raiser, to discuss these consequences. Donors should obtain their own tax advice.)

The types of gifts that can lead to private foundation status are basically any large gift from an individual, company, or private foundation and any gift from so-called disqualified persons: officers, directors, and trustees of the charity, their relatives, and businesses with which they are associated, and previous donors of large gifts. (The definitions of these types of gifts are complex and the exact language of the Internal Revenue Code, in Section 509(a), should be consulted.) While a fund raiser may seek such gifts, he or she should do so with an awareness of the tax rules and of when additional professional advice is needed.

10A.4 REFERENCES

American Institute of Certified Public Accountants (AICPA). *Accounting Principles and Reporting Practices for Certain Nonprofit Organizations.* Statement of Position No. 78-10. New York: AICPA, 1978.

American Institute of Certified Public Accountants. *Accounting for Joint Costs of Informational Materials and Activities of Not-for-Profit Organizations That Include a Fund-Raising Appeal.* Statement of Position No. 87-2. New York: AICPA, 1987.

American Institute of Certified Public Accountants. *Accounting for Costs of Materials and Activities of Not-for-Profit Organizations and State and Local Governmental Entities That Include a Fund-Raising Appeal.* (Exposure drafts). New York: AICPA, 1993a.

American Institute of Certified Public Accountants. *Reporting of Related Entities by Not-for-Profit Organizations.* New York: AICPA, 1993b.

Financial Accounting Standards Board (FASB). *Accounting for Contributions Received and Contributions Made.* Statement of Financial Accounting Standards No. 116. Norwalk, Conn.: FASB, 1993a.

Financial Accounting Standards Board. *Financial Statements of Not-for-Profit Organizations.* Statement of Financial Accounting Standards No. 117. Norwalk, Conn.: FASB, 1993b.

PART TWO

Financial Statement Presentation

CHAPTER 11

Cash Basis Financial Statements

p. 161. ***Add at bottom of page:***
Also note the guidance in Chapter 3 of this supplement as to appropriate disclosures in cash basis financial statements.

CHAPTER 13

Multiclass Financial Statements

13.1 STATEMENT OF FINANCIAL ACCOUNTING STANDARDS NO. 117—*FINANCIAL STATEMENTS OF NOT-FOR-PROFIT ORGANIZATIONS*

p. 189. *Add after third paragraph:*

Note that some not-for-profit organizations receive types of revenue that do have legal restrictions attached to them, but, because the restrictions are not placed by a *donor* on a *gift* to the organization, the revenue (and any unspent related net assets) are reported in the *un*restricted class of net assets. Examples of such revenue include: student dormitory fees at a university, which must be deposited into a sinking fund to be used to repay bonds issued to build the dormitory; a portion of dues paid to a labor union, which must be retained in a separate strike fund for use only to pay benefits to striking members; a special assessment on members of a country club, to be used only for the cost of a new swimming pool; revenue of an annual church fair specified for addition to the organization's building fund; royalties from licensing of an organization's logo, which are to be used only for the organization's homeless shelter program.

In these cases the restrictions arise from the bond indenture, the constitution of the labor union, the formal resolution approved by the country club members authorizing the special assessment, the previous vote of the church vestry that the fair proceeds will be put in the building fund, and the contract with the organization that purchased the rights to use the organization's logo, respectively. These are very real restrictions which must be adhered to; they just did not arise in the context of gifts. Therefore they do not create revenue which is reported in one of the restricted classes as defined in SFAS No. 117.

(e) Statement of Cash Flows

p. 192. ***Add at end of subsection:***

Following is a practical guide to preparation of a statement of cash flows. It starts with the balance sheet and statement of financial activity for a hypothetical small not-for-profit organization. Next are two worksheets used to create the statement of cash flows, accompanied by explanations of the worksheets.

SAMPLE PERFORMING ARTS ORGANIZATION
BALANCE SHEET ($000)

	June 30	
Assets	19X2	19X1
Cash	$ 116	$ 169
Short-term investments	154	151
Accounts receivable, net of allowance	70	28
Grants receivable	28	6
Long-term investments, at market value	180	156
Property and equipment, net of depreciation	155	140
Rent and other deposits	4	9
Other assets	11	13
Total assets	$ 718	$ 672
Liabilities and Net Assets		
Accounts payable and accrued expenses	$ 111	$ 66
Deferred season subscription revenue	206	193
Current portion of mortgage	30	30
Mortgage payable, 8%, due 19X4	29	59
Commitments and contingencies (Note x)	—	—
Total liabilities	376	348
Net Assets:		
Unrestricted:		
Designated by the board for endowment	82	66
Equity in property and equipment	96	51
Undesignated, available for operations	35	94
Total unrestricted net assets	213	211
Temporarily restricted:		
Expendable	31	23
Nonexpendable	21	21
Total temporarily restricted net assets	52	44
Permanently restricted net assets	77	69
Total net assets	342	324
Total liabilities and net assets	$ 718	$ 672

SAMPLE PERFORMING ARTS ORGANIZATION
STATEMENT OF FINANCIAL ACTIVITY ($000)
YEAR ENDED JUNE 30, 19X2

	Unrestricted	Temporarily Restricted	Permanently Restricted	Total
Operating revenue:				
Ticket sales	$ 857			$ 857
Other performance fees	128			128
Concessions	103			103
Investment income	21	$ 2		23
Gains/losses on investments	55		$ 4	59
Net assets released from restrictions	188	(188)	—	-
Total operating revenue	1352	(186)	4	1170
Operating expenses:				
Regular season productions	815			815
Ballet school	201			201
Other productions	378			378
Production administration	497			497
Management and general	390			390
Total operating expenses	2281	—	—	2281
Deficiency from operations	(929)	(186)	4	(1111)
Support:				
Annual giving	584	39		623
Grants	140	125		265
Endowment gifts			4	4
Governments	200	30		230
Donated services and materials	43			43
Less: Fund-raising costs	(36)	—	—	(36)
Net support	931	194	4	1129
Change in net assets:				
Unrestricted	2			2
Temporarily restricted		8		8
Permanently restricted			8	8
Total change in net assets				18
Net Assets:				
Beginning of year	211	44	69	324
End of year	$ 213	$ 52	$ 77	$ 342

(Complete comparative prior year information can be presented on a separate page, or a total column for the prior year added at the right side of this page.)

SAMPLE PERFORMING ARTS ORGANIZATION
STATEMENT OF CASH FLOWS ($000)

	Year ended June 30	
	19X2	19X1
Cash flows from operating activities:		
Cash received from ticket sales	$ 870	$ 685
Cash received from contributors	1,079	1,208
Interest and dividends received	23	27
Cash received from other revenue sources	189	72
Cash paid to employees and suppliers	(2,190)	(1,931)
Interest paid	(5)	(7)
Net cash provided (used) by operating activities	(34)	54
Cash flows from investing activities:		
Purchase of equipment	(25)	(31)
Proceeds from sale of equipment	-	16
Purchase of investments	(84)	(108)
Proceeds from sale of investments	116	(65)
Net cash provided (used) by investing activities	7	(58)
Cash flows from financing activities:		
Proceeds from contributions restricted for:		
Investment in endowment	4	27
Investment in property and equipment	-	31
Other financing activities:		
Payments on mortgage	(30)	(30)
Net cash provided (used) by financing activities	(26)	28
Net increase (decrease) in cash	(53)	24
Cash at beginning of year	169	145
Cash at end of year	$ 116	$ 169
Supplemental data for noncash investing and financing activities:		
Gifts of equipment	$ 10	$ 6
Gift of paid-up life insurance, cash surrender value	7	

RECONCILIATION OF CHANGE IN NET ASSETS TO NET CASH PROVIDED (USED) BY OPERATING ACTIVITIES

Change in Net Assets	$ 18
Adjustments to reconcile change in net assets to net cash used by operating activities:	
Noncash revenues and expenses:	
Depreciation	20
Net realized and unrealized gain on long-term investments	(59)
Noncash contributions of long-term assets:	
Equipment	10
Life insurance policy	7
Nonexpendable endowment gift	(4)
Changes in current assets and liabilities:	
Increase in accounts receivable	(42)
Increase in grants receivable	(22)
Decrease in rent and other deposits	5
Decrease in other assets	9
Increase in accounts payable	45
Increase in deferred revenue	13
Net cash used by operating activities	$ (34)

Explanation of Cash Flow Statement Worksheets

Following is a summary of the process for preparing a statement of cash flows, using the direct method, from two balance sheets and the corresponding income statement. The only additional information required, which will not be obvious from those statements, is:

- Gross amounts of acquisitions and dispositions of long-term assets and liabilities; these data should be available from the general ledger or the investment ledger.
- Information to identify changes in each of the various current assets and liabilities with their related revenue or expense (operating cash inflow or outflow) categories. This information will be available either from the general ledger, the accounting manual, or the bookkeeper's knowledge of the organization.

Most prepaid expenses and accounts payable will normally relate to the "payments to employees and suppliers" category. Some receivable and deferred revenue items are obvious: grants receivable relate to grant revenue (entry 7 in the reclassification column). Some will require further investigation. For example, in the sample worksheet, the change in accounts receivable is entirely related to performance fee revenue (reclassification entry 6), but this is not obvious from looking at only the financial statements. In some cases, one balance sheet item may relate to more than one income statement item, and the change must be allocated among the various income statement items.

A. Paste comparative balance sheets on worksheet. Details of net assets by class are not needed and can be removed to save space. Total assets and liabilities are not used; total net assets is.

B. Subtract the prior period numbers from the current period numbers, line by line, including the total change in net assets. Record the difference as either positive or negative according to the usual rules for debits and credits (i.e., increases in assets are debits, increases in liabilities and net assets are credits, etc.). In the difference column, debits are written as positive numbers; credits (including an increase in net assets) as negative numbers. Foot the column of differences; it must foot to zero.

C. Paste the statement of activity below the balance sheet so the total column lines up under the balance sheet difference column. Details of changes in net assets by class, and beginning and ending net assets, are not required; total change in net assets is.

D. Depending on the convention used in the statement of activity regarding signs, it may be necessary to change some of the signs from positive to negative so that all credit numbers (i.e., revenue) are negative and all debit numbers (expenses) are positive, consistent with the signs of the balance sheet differences. However, do not change the sign of the total change in net assets ($18), as this is a balancing number. If it is an increase, it will be a positive number, and vice versa; leave it as it is. Note especially items that have been reported as deductions from other numbers (the $36 of fund-raising costs in the example) so that their signs are correct (double negative = positive (i.e., a debit), in the example). Foot this entire column, including the total change in net assets (with the proper sign, as previously noted). This column must also add to zero.

E. Reclassify items to put them into the proper categories for the statement of cash flows. The number of reclassification columns is not fixed; it should be based on how complex a set of statements you have and how many entries there will be. In the example, there are two columns: one for items affecting only one of the statements, and one for items affecting both statements. These columns may be further subdivided if more space is needed to post entries.

In general, reclassify balance sheet items related to operating cash flows (typically, all current assets and liabilities, and some others) out of the balance sheet section to the related revenue or expense line item. Explanations of the various reclassification entries are on the following page.

Be very careful with signs here. Many of the entries will have the effect of zeroing out one of the lines; that part of the entry will have the sign necessary to offset the number(s) already on that line; the other part of the entry will have the opposite sign. (If it is desired to zero out a line with a positive number on it, such as the accounts receivable line with a positive $42 in Column B, a negative $42 entry (entry 6) is required on that line. The other part of entry 6, on the "other performance fees" line, must have a positive sign, and vice versa.)

F. Foot each reclassification column. They must all foot to zero.

G. Take a subtotal at this point to ensure that everything balances and to present most of the actual numbers that will end up on the statement of cash flows. Foot this column; it must foot to zero.

H. Gross up those items involving acquisition and disposition of long-term assets and liabilities. Usual items include investments (those that are not cash equivalents), fixed assets, and long-term debt. There may be others. Information needed to generate the gross-up amounts will be available in the general ledger or (in the case of investments) from the organization's investment manager.

I. Carry each item from Column H, and from the gross-up columns, *except the change in cash and cash equivalents* ($53), into the appropriate column (operating, investing, financing) for the statement of cash flows. *Change all signs at this point: all negative numbers become positive, and vice versa,* to show the item with the sign the item will have in the actual statement. Positive items are cash inflows; negative items are cash outflows.

Items (other than the change in cash and cash equivalents) still left in the balance sheet (upper) part of the worksheet are investing or financing cash flows. Any grossed-up items must be copied gross to show both acquisitions and dispositions. Items in the income statement (lower) part of the worksheet are mostly operating cash flows, except for contributions restricted for nonexpendable purposes ($4 endowment gift in the example), which are financing cash flows. Foot the three columns to produce the net cash flows from each category; the sum of the three footings—($34), $7, ($26)—must equal the change in cash—($53) (see bottom of cash flow columns).

J. Certain items require special treatment:

- The change in cash and cash equivalents is merely copied to the statement of cash flows *without changing its sign* (as this is also a balancing number.)

- Noncash financing and investing items do not appear in the body of the statement, but are disclosed separately below. These items are identified during the reclassification process (step E, entries 9 and 12 in the example.)

Now you are ready to draft the actual statement of cash flows, using the numbers in the last four columns of the worksheet.

Explanation of Reclassification Entries for Statement of Cash Flows

1. To group change in short-term investments (other than those which are cash equivalents; these are included with cash) with change in long-term investments.
2. To move change in long-term portion of mortgage to the line related to the actual payment made, i.e. the current portion. (This entry is really just a formality, and need not be made.)
3. To break interest paid (required separate disclosure) out of operating expenses. Number obtained from general ledger.
4. To offset noncash donation against the expense reflecting use of the donated item. (Note: this does not appear as part of the supplemental disclosure of noncash transactions, because it is an operating item, not financing or investing.) Number obtained from contribution records.
5. To include fund-raising costs (reported as an offset against contributions) with other cash expenses.
6. To adjust performance fee revenue for change in related receivables.
7. To adjust grant revenue for change in related receivable.
8. To reclassify gain on sale of investments to the investment line.
9. To reduce contribution revenue and the change in fixed assets by the amount of donated fixed assets. (This is one of the supplemental noncash items disclosed, because it is an investing transaction.) Number obtained from contribution records.
10. To reclassify depreciation expense to the fixed assets line. Number obtained from general ledger.
11. To adjust operating expenses for the change in prepaid expenses.
12. To reduce contributions, and change in other assets, by the amount of the donated life insurance policy. Number obtained from contribution records. This is also a separate disclosure item.
13. To adjust operating expenses for the change in other assets. Note that this entry cannot be made until after entry 12, as this is really a plug to zero out the change in other assets, *after* reflecting the change due to the life insurance policy, which must be treated separately because it is a noncash item.

WORKSHEET FOR STATEMENT OF

Balance Sheet [A]	Current	Prior	[B]	[Dr. (Cr.)] Balance sheet Changes
Cash	$116	$169		(53)
Short-term investments	154	151		3
Accounts receivable, net of allowance	70	28		42
Grants receivable	28	6		22
Long-term investments, at market value	180	156		24
Property and equipment, net of depreciation	155	140		15
Rent and other deposits	4	9		(5)
Other assets	11	13		(2)
Accounts payable and accrued expenses	$111	$ 66		(45)
Deferred season subscription revenue	206	193		(13)
Current portion of mortgage	30	30		-0-
Mortgage payable, 8%, due 19X3	29	59		30
Total net assets	342	324		(18)
				- 0 -

Income Statement: [C]	Unrestricted	Temporarily Restricted	Permanently Restricted	Total
Operating revenue:				
Ticket sales	$857		[D]	$(857)
Other performance fees	128			(128)
Concessions	103			(103)
Investment income	21	$ 2		(23)
Gains/losses on investments	55		$4	(59)
Net assets released from restrictions	188	(188)	—	-
Operating expenses:				
Regular season productions	815			815
Ballet school	201			201
Other productions	378			378
Production administration	497			497
Management and general	390			390
Total operating expenses	2,281	—	—	2,281
Interest				
Support:				
Annual giving	584	39		(623)
Grants	140	125		(265)
Endowment gifts			4	(4)
Governments	200	30		(230)
Donated services and materials	43			(43)
Less: Fund-raising costs	(36)	—	—	((36))
Change in net assets	2	8	8	18
				-0-

Noncash financing and investing items (memo)):

CASH FLOWS—DIRECT METHOD

[E] Reclassifications: Within B/S or P/L	Reclassifications: Between B/S & P/L	[G] Subtotal	Gross-up: Purchases	[H] Gross-up: Sales	[I] [Source (Use)] Statement of Cash Flows: Operating	Investing	Financing	Other [J]
		(53)						(53)
[1](3)		-0-						
	[6](42)	-0-						
	[7](22)	-0-				[(84)		
[1]3	[8](59)	(32)	84	(116)		-[116		
	[9](10) 20[10]	25				(25)		
	[11]5	-0-						
	[12](7) 9[13]	-0-						
	[14]45	-0-						
	[15]13	-0-						
[2]30		30					(30)	
[2](30)		-0-						
	[16]18	-0-						
	[15](13)	(870)			870			
	[6]42]-	(189)			189			
	]							
		(23)			23			
	[8]59	-0-						
-[[4](43)	[10](20)]							
[[5]36	[11](5)]-	2,190			(2,190)			
[[3](5)	13(9)]							
	[14](45)]							
[3]5		5			(5)			
	[12]7]							
	[9]10]							
	[7]22]-	(1,079)			1,079			
		(4)					4	
	]							
[4]43		-0-						
[5](36)		-0-						
	[16](18)	-0-						
-0-	-0-	-0-			(34)	+ 7	+ (26)	= (53)

[F]

[9]10		Equipment	$ 10
[12]7		Life insurance	7

WORKSHEET FOR RECONCILIATION

	Current	Prior	B	[Dr. (Cr.)] Balance sheet Changes
Balance Sheet				
Cash	$116	$169		(53)
Short-term investments	154	151		3
Accounts receivable, net of allowance	70	28		42
Grants receivable	28	6		22
Long-term investments, at market value	180	156		24
Property and equipment, net of depreciation	155	140		15
Rent and other deposits	4	9		(5)
Other assets	11	13		(2)
A				
Accounts payable and accrued expenses	$111	$ 66		(45)
Deferred season subscription revenue	206	193		(13)
Current portion of mortgage	30	30		-0-
Mortgage payable, 8%, due 19X3	29	59		30
Total net assets	342	324		(18)
				-0-

Items to reconcile to operating cash flows:

Gain on sale

Depreciation

Noncash contributions:

Equipment

Life insurance

Services and materials

Expense representing use of donated services and materials

Nonexpendable gift

Financing cash flow—nonexpendable gift

(Steps C, D not used)

TO OPERATING CASH FLOWS

E	F	G	H		I	[Source (Use)]	J
Reclassifications					Statement of Cash Flows		
Within	Between	Subtotal	Gross-up			Financing/	
B/S or P/L	B/S & P/L		Purchases	Sales	Operating	Investing	Other
		(53)					(53)
[1](3)		-					
		42			(42)		
		22			(22)		
[1]3	[8](59)	(32)	84	(116)		32	
	[9](10) 20[10]	25				(25)	
		(5)			5		
	[12](7)	(9)			9		
		(45)			45		
		(13)			13		
[2]30		30				(30)	
[2](30)		-					
		(18)			18		
	[8]59	59			(59)		
	[10](20)	(20)			20		
	[9]10	10			(10)		
	[12]7	7			(7)		
[4]43							
		-0-					
[4](43)							
[17]4		4			(4)		
[17](4)		(4)				4	
-0-	-0-	-0-			(34) +	(19) =	(53)
						F - (26)	
						I - 7	
						(19)	

14. To adjust operating expenses by the change in payables and accruals.
15. To adjust ticket sale revenue by the amount of the change in deferred ticket revenue.
16. To offset the two changes in total net assets numbers.

These entries are illustrative only; not all will be required for every organization and additional entries will be required for many organizations.

Explanation of "Reconciliation" Worksheet

Steps A and B are the same as for the first worksheet. A copy of that part of that worksheet can be pasted on this worksheet. The statement of activity is not used for this worksheet.

The reclassification columns include some, but not all, of the entries from the first worksheet. Many of these entries are to create the reconciling items between change in net assets and operating cash flows.

One additional entry is included:

17. To reclassify nonexpendable gifts to the financing cash flows category.

(On the first worksheet, this was done as part of the drafting of the statement of cash flows itself.)

Entries not included here are those to reclassify changes in current assets and liabilities to the respective revenue and expense categories (entries 6, 7, 11, 13, 14, and 15), to reclassify certain revenue and expense items (entries 3 and 5), and to offset the change in net assets (entry 16).

Note that entry 4 (the $43 gift of services and materials) does appear here. However, because it affects contribution revenue and operating expenses, both of which are part of operating cash flows, the two parts of this entry offset each other and the results of the entry disappear.

As before, all columns through the subtotal (Column G) must foot to zero, and when carrying the items from this column to the statement of cash flows (Columns I), all signs except cash are changed (plus to minus, and vice versa).

The items in the operating column of the statement of cash flows now include:

- all changes in current assets and liabilities,
- the change in net assets ($18 in the example), and
- the reconciling items referred to earlier.

This column must foot to the same amount as net cash flows from operations on the first worksheet - ($34) in the example.

The financing/investing cash flow column is included here only as proof that the worksheet has been accurately prepared. Items that are not part of the operating cash flow column are carried to this column; the total of this column must equal the sum of those two categories on the first worksheet, and this total plus the net operating cash flow amount must equal the change in cash - ($53).

If it is desired to present the statement of cash flows using the indirect method (not recommended), then the reconciliation prepared on the second worksheet replaces the operating cash flow section of the statement as shown. (The investing and financing sections of the statement are the same as before.) The first worksheet is not needed; the gross-up information (Columns H) can be included on the second worksheet. An additional separate disclosure required in this case is the amount of interest paid ($5 in the example).

SAMPLE ________ ORGANIZATION
STATEMENT OF CASH FLOWS ($000)

YEAR ENDED ___

	19__	19__
Cash flows from operating activities:		
Cash received from ticket sales	$	$
Cash received from contributors		
Interest and dividends received		
Cash received from other revenue sources		
Cash paid to employees and suppliers		
Interest paid	___	___
Net cash provided (used) by operating activities	___	___
Cash flows from investing activities:		
Purchase of equipment		
Proceeds from sale of equipment		
Purchase of investments		
Proceeds from sale of investments	___	___
Net cash provided (used) by investing activities	___	___
Cash flows from financing activities:		
Proceeds from contributions restricted for:		
Investment in endowment		
Investment in property and equipment		
Other financing activities:		
Payments on mortgage	___	___
Net cash provided (used) by financing activities	___	___
Net increase (decrease) in cash		
Cash at beginning of year	___	___
Cash at end of year	$ ___	$ ___
Supplemental data for noncash investing and financing activities:		
Gifts of equipment	$	$
Gift of paid-up life insurance, cash surrender value		

RECONCILIATION OF CHANGE IN NET ASSETS TO NET CASH PROVIDED (USED) BY OPERATING ACTIVITIES

Change in Net Assets	$
Adjustments to reconcile change in net assets to net cash used by operating activities:	
Noncash revenues and expenses:	
Depreciation	
Net realized and unrealized gain on long-term investments	
Noncash contributions of long-term assets:	
Equipment	
Life insurance policy	
Nonexpendable endowment gift	
Changes in current assets and liabilities:	
Increase in accounts receivable	
Increase in grants receivable	
Decrease in rent and other deposits	
Decrease in other assets	
Increase in accounts payable	
Increase in deferred revenue	
Net cash used by operating activities	$

WORKSHEET FOR STATEMENT OF

Balance Sheet [A]	Current	Prior	[B]	[Dr. (Cr.)] Balance sheet Changes
Cash	$	$		
Short-term investments				
Accounts receivable, net of allowance				
Grants receivable				
Long-term investments, at market value				
Property and equipment, net of depreciation				
Rent and other deposits				
Other assets	____	____		
Accounts payable and accrued expenses	$	$		
Deferred season subscription revenue				
Current portion of mortgage				-0-
Mortgage payable, 8%, due 19X3	____	____		
Total net assets	____	____		- 0 -

Income Statement: [C]	Unrestricted	Temporarily Restricted	Permanently Restricted	Total
Operating revenue:				
Ticket sales	$		[D] $	
Other performance fees				
Concessions				
Investment income		$		
Gains/losses on investments			$	
Net assets released from restrictions	____	(___)	____	-
Operating expenses:				
Regular season productions				
Ballet school				
Other productions				
Production administration				
Management and general	____			____
Total operating expenses	____	____	____	____
Interest				
Support:				
Annual giving				
Grants				
Endowment gifts				
Governments				
Donated services and materials				
Less: Fund-raising costs	____	____	____	(( ))
Change in net assets	____	____	____	-0-

Noncash financing and investing items (memo):

CASH FLOWS—DIRECT METHOD

[E] Reclassifications Within B/S or P/L	Between B/S & P/L	[G] Subtotal	[H] Gross-up Purchases	Sales	[I] [Source (Use)] Statement of Cash Flows Operating	Investing	Financing	Other [J]
1		-0-						
	6	-0-						
	7	-0-				[		
1	8					-[		
	9 10							
	11	-0-						
	12 13	-0-						
	14	-0-						
	15	-0-						
2								
2		-0-						
	16	-0-						
	15							
	6]-							
	]							
	8	-0-						
-[4	10]							
[5	11]-							
[3	13]							
	14]							
3								
	12]							
	9]							
	7]-							
	]							
4		-0-						
		-0-						
	16	-0-						
-0-	-0-	-0-			___ +	___ +	___ =	___

[F]

9	Equipment	$
12	Life insurance	

WORKSHEET FOR RECONCILIATION

	Current	Prior	B	[Dr. (Cr.)] Balance sheet Changes
Balance Sheet				
Cash	$	$		
Short-term investments				
Accounts receivable, net of allowance				
Grants receivable				
Long-term investments, at market value				
Property and equipment, net of depreciation				
Rent and other deposits				
Other assets				
	A			
Accounts payable and accrued expenses	$	$		
Deferred season subscription revenue				
Current portion of mortgage				
Mortgage payable, 8%, due 19X3				
Total net assets				
				-0-
Items to reconcile to operating cash flows:				
Gain on sale				
Depreciation				
Noncash contributions:				
Equipment				
Life insurance				
Services and materials				
Expense representing use of donated services and materials				
Nonexpendable gift				
Financing cash flow—nonexpendable gift				

(Steps C, D not used)

TO OPERATING CASH FLOWS

E	F	G	H		I	[Source (Use)]	J
Reclassifications					Statement of Cash Flows		
Within B/S or P/L	Between B/S & P/L	Subtotal	Gross-up Purchases	Sales	Operating	Financing/ Investing	Other
1		-					
1	8						
	9 10						
	12						
2							
2		-					
	8						
	10 ( )	( )					
	9						
	12						
4							
		-0-					
4							
17							
17							
-0-	-0-	-0-				+	=
						F -	
						I -	

PART THREE

Accounting and Reporting Guidelines

CHAPTER 14

Voluntary Health and Welfare Organizations

p. 219. *Add after second paragraph:*
As of late 1995, the AICPA has issued an exposure draft of the new audit guide. A summary of its proposed provisions appears in Appendix D of this supplement.

14.3 ACCOUNTING FOR CONTRIBUTIONS

p. 225. *Add before subsection (2):*
See the discussion of pass-through gifts at Section 9.2(a) of this supplement.

14.4 ACCOUNTING FOR OTHER INCOME

(b) Gains or Losses on Invetments

p. 229. *Add after first full paragraph:*
See the discussion of the FASB statement on accounting for losses on restricted endowment funds in Chapter 8 of this supplement.

14.6 ACCOUNTING FOR ASSETS

(a) Carrying Value of Investments

p. 232. *Add after first paragraph in subsection:*
See the discussion of the FASB statement on accounting for marketable securities in Chapter 8 of this supplement. Briefly, it requires such investments to be reported at current fair market value.

(b) Fixed Asset Accounting

p. 234. *Add at end of subection:*
This method is discussed in the new AICPA audit guide exposure draft (see Appendix D). See also the discussion of gifts of the use of property in Section 10.2(d).

14.8 FINANCIAL STATEMENTS

(c) Reporting of Expenses

p. 243. *Add at end of fourth paragraph:*
This new SOP expected to be issued before the end of 1996.

(f) Statement of Cash Flows (Formerly Changes in Financial Position)

p. 249. *Add at end of subsection:*
Chapter 13 of this supplement contains a practical guide for preparation of a statement of cash flows.

(g) Statement of Functional Expenses

p. 249. *Add after first paragraph of subsection:*
SFAS No. 117 requires voluntary health and welfare organizations to present a statement of functional expenses. Other types of not-for-profit organizations are encouraged to present this statement, but are not required to do so.

14.10 THE EVOLUTION OF STANDARDS

p. 250. *Add at end of first full paragraph:*
The new edition of the Black Book is expected to be issued in 1996.

CHAPTER 15

Colleges and Universities

15.1 AUTHORITATIVE PRONOUNCEMENTS

(a) AICPA Audit Guide

p. 258. ***Add at end of subsection:***
As of late 1995, the AICPA had issued an exposure draft of a new audit guide that will supersede the college audit guide. A summary of its proposed provisions appears in Appendix D of this supplement.

15.4 ACCOUNTING PRINCIPLES

(h) Gains or Losses on Investments

p. 274. ***Add at end of subsection:***
See the discussion, in Chapter 8 of this supplement, of the FASB statement on accounting for losses on restricted endowment funds.

(i) Carrying Value of Investments

p. 274. *Add at end of subsection:*
See the discussion, in Chapter 8 of this supplement, of the FASB statement on accounting for marketable securities. Briefly, it requires such investments to be reported at current fair market value.

CHAPTER 16

Health Care Providers

16.2 AUTHORITATIVE PRONOUNCMENTS

(a) AICPA Audit Guide

p. 279. *Add at end of third paragraph:*
As of late 1995, the AICPA had issued an exposure draft of this new guide. It is expected to be issued as a final guide in 1996.

16.3 FUND ACCOUNTING

(a) Unrestricted Net Assets

p. 281. *Replace last sentence of subsection with:*
Such funds would be required to be disclosed separately from assets whose use is externally limited.

16.4 FINANCIAL STATEMENTS

(a) Balance Sheet

p. 283. ***Replace second paragraph of subsection with:***

SFAS No. 117 requires that information about liquidity of assets and liabilities be provided in the balance sheet. Unlike many other types of not-for-profit organizations, many health care entities traditionally have prepared a classified balance sheet—that is, one in which assets and liabilities are catagorized as current or noncurrent. The proposed new guide is expected to require all providers to meet the liquidity requirements by preparing a classified balance sheet.

p. 287. ***Change (c) Statement of Cash Flows of General Funds to:***

(c) Statement of Cash Flows

p. 287. ***Delete first paragraph of subsection.***

p. 287. ***Add after second paragraph:***

Chapter 13 of this supplement contains a practical guide for preparation of a statement of cash flows.

16.5 ACCOUNTING PRINCIPLES

(a) Generally Accepted Accounting Principles

p. 287. ***Replace first sentence of subsection with:***

Financial statements of health care entities should be prepared in accordance with generally accepted accounting principles.

(g) Investments

p. 292. ***Insert before first sentence of subsection:***

Guidance as to how providers should account for and report investments is expected to change upon issuance of the proposed new audit guide. However, until that guide is finalized, the following guidance is in effect.

p. 293. ***Add at end of subsection:***

See the discussion, in Chapter 8 of this supplement, of the FASB statement on accounting for marketable securities and losses on restricted endowments. It requires such investments to be reported in the balance sheet at current fair market value.

CHAPTER 17

Accounting Standards for Other Not-for-Profit Organizations

p. 299. ***Add after third full paragraph:***
As of late 1995, the AICPA had issued an exposure draft of the new audit guide, which will supersede Statement of Position No. 78-10. A summary of the draft's proposed provisions appears in Appendix D of this supplement.

17.1 ACCOUNTING PRINCIPLES

(j) Gains and Losses

p. 304. ***Add after third paragraph:***
See the discussion, in Chapter 8 of this supplement, of the FASB statement on accounting for losses on restricted endowment funds.

p. 305. ***Add at end of carryover paragraph:***
See Section 17.1(m) in this supplement.

(m) Reported Valuation of Investment

p. 307. *Add at end of subsection:*
See the discussion, in Chapter 8 of this supplement, of the FASB statement on accounting for marketable securities. Briefly, it requires such investments to be reported at current fair market value.

17.2 FINANCIAL STATEMENTS

(g) Statement of Cash Flows (Formerly Changes in Financial Position)

p. 313. *Add at end of subsection:*
Chapter 13 of this supplement contains a practical guide for preparation of a statement of cash flows.

17.3 COMBINED FINANCIAL STATEMENTS

(b) Funds Held in Trust by Others

p. 314. *Add at end of subsection:*
See Section 10.3 in this supplement for further discussion of this topic.

CHAPTER 18

Special Accounting Problems of Specific Organizations

18.1 ASSOCIATIONS AND PROFESSIONAL SOCIETIES

(a) Reporting on a Functional Basis

p. 320. *Add at end of subsection:*
See Section 2.2(f) in this supplement for a discussion of what the proposed AICPA audit guide says about whether associations must report expenses on a functional basis.

18.3 CLUBS

p. 324. *Add at end of carryover paragraph:*
See Section 2.2(f) in this supplement for a discussion of what the proposed AICPA audit guide says about whether clubs must follow accounting principles for not-for-profit organizations.

18.7 PRIVATE FOUNDATIONS

(b) Investments at Market

p. 334. ***Add at end of subsection:***
See the discussion, in Chapter 8 of this supplement, of the FASB statement on accounting for marketable securities. Briefly, it requires such investments to be reported at current fair market value.

18.8 RELIGIOUS ORGANIZATIONS OTHER THAN CHURCHES

(b) Allocations from Other Organizations

p. 336. ***Add at end of subsection:***
See also the discussion of pass-through gifts in Section 9.2(a) in this supplement.

CHAPTER 19

The Financial Accounting Standards Board and Future Trends in Not-For-Profit Accounting

19.1 FINANCIAL ACCOUNTING STANDARDS BOARD

(a) Establishment of Accounting Rules

p. 343. *Add at end of subsection:*

As of late 1995, the AICPA had issued exposure drafts of two new audit guides, which will supersede the audit guides discussed in Chapters 14–16 and Statement of Position No. 78-10. A summary of the proposed provisions of one of the guides appears in Appendix D of this supplement.

(c) FASB Not-For-Profit Projects

p. 345. ***Add at end of subsection:***
In late 1995, the FASB issued a new statement of financial accounting standards on accounting for investments. Its provisions are discussed in Chapter 8 of this supplement.

(d) AICPA Projects

p. 345. ***Add at end of first paragraph in subsection:***
See Section 19.1(a) in this supplement.

p. 346. ***Add at end of carryover paragraph:***
This new SOP is expected to be issued before the end of 1996.

19.2 TRENDS IN NOT-FOR-PROFIT ACCOUNTING

(b) Reporting Certain Assets at Current Value

p. 347. ***Add at end of subsection:***
SFAS No. 124 does just that. See the discussion in Chapter 8 of this supplement.

PART FOUR

Controlling the Not-for-Profit Organization

CHAPTER 20

The Importance of Budgeting

20.1 THE BUDGET: A PLAN OF ACTION

(b) Levels of Resources

p. 359. ***Add at end of last bullet:***
(See Myth No. 21 in Chapter 1A of this supplement.)

p. 360. ***Add after first full paragraph:***

An example of an organization that must be prepared to respond very quickly to large, unpredictable demands on its resources is the American Red Cross. When disaster strikes, they must be ready to help—immediately. They cannot sit back and wait, and then go out and raise some extra money after the disaster happens. Thus, for them a desirable level of reserves is much larger (maybe as much as two years' normal budget) than for most organizations. Donors can be presumed to understand this, and not be reluctant to contribute.

Similarly, a museum that wishes to able to acquire new items for its collection must have the financial resources available when the opportunity arises. If a desirable painting is coming up at auction next week, and the museum can't afford to bid on the painting, it will be unable to acquire it for the collection.

In contrast, a local day care center, with very predictable expenses, and a long-term contract for funding from a reliable revenue source, does not normally need as much in the way of reserves.

CHAPTER 23

Small Organizations—Providing Internal Control

23.1 REASONS FOR INTERNAL CONTROL

p. 404. ***Add at end of section:***
For example, several recent, real, well-publicized situations involving not-for-profit organizations were all at least partly due to the absence of adequate internal controls:

- The chief executive officer of a major charity misused some of the organization's funds for personal benefit. If this person had been subject to adequate oversight and review by the organization's board of directors, the amount of money that could have been misused probably would have been only a small fraction of what the organization eventually lost.
- The chief financial officer of a national organization embezzled money from the organization's bank accounts and covered up the theft by making improper entries in the books. Had this person been subject to adequate control, including proper segregation of duties, enforced by the organization's board and chief executive, the thefts would likely not have happened at all, or, if money had been taken, the loss would have been evident to others more quickly.
- A similar situation occurred at a major museum, but was not detected until a new chief executive arrived and became suspicious.

- Another chief executive spent the organization's money on personal expenses and on projects that were not subject to adequate review and approval by the board. Had the board been more aware of what was happening, these wasteful expenditures could have been minimized, or possibly avoided altogether.
- A large religious organization entered into contracts which created liabilities that it had no ability to fulfill. The chief executive did this on his own, without proper board supervision and review.
- A charity that promised to match amounts placed with it by donors and other charities may have been simply a fraud run by its chief executive. Again, if the board had realized what was really going on, things presumably would not have gotten as far out of hand as they did.
- (Although governments are not the type of not-for-profit mainly discussed in this book, this organization's story could happen in a not-for-profit as well.) The treasurer of a local government invested its cash reserves in extremely speculative investments, which eventually turned sour. The government was forced into bankruptcy. If the governing board had exercised stronger controls over the investment activities of the treasurer, the speculative investments would have been much less likely to have resulted in the large losses that occurred.

This is not in any way to condone or excuse the actions of the individuals who did things they should not have done; however, the fact that they were able to do what they did, over a period of time, without being promptly called to account for their actions, indicates that those in positions of responsibility over these individuals were not adequately discharging their responsibilities for guarding the organizations' resources. In fact, the very presence of adequate internal controls might have deterred some of these people from even attempting to do anything improper. Note that we are not talking here about taking $50 from the petty cash fund. Of course a board (or a chief executive) has more important things to do than worry about that (that's the controller's job). These were situations so significant that the very existence of the organizations and their programs were called into question. That is surely a major concern of the very top officials of an organization.

Further, in every case, the ultimate harm to the organization extended far beyond the actual amount of money stolen or wasted. Each situation became a public relations disaster; three ended up in bankruptcy court; some people have gone to jail. When the not-for-profit organizations' donors finally became aware of what had happened, contributions dropped significantly. The loss of contributions can never be measured precisely, of course, but it was doubtless many times the actual amount that triggered the donors' reactions. It can take many years for an organization's finances to recover from such a debacle, if they ever do.

CHAPTER 23 A (NEW)

Effective Internal Accounting Control for Not-for-Profit Organizations

23A.1 INTRODUCTION TO INTERNAL ACCOUNTING CONTROL

(a) Definition

Accounting literature defines internal accounting control as the

- plan of organization,
- procedures, and
- records

designed to enhance the *safeguarding* of assets and the *reliability of financial* records of an organization. Internal accounting control provides reasonable, but not absolute, assurance that:

- transactions conform with management authorization;
- transactions are recorded in accordance with accounting conventions, and accountability over assets is maintained;
- access to assets is limited to authorized persons;
- periodic comparison of asset records and existing assets would disclose significant discrepancies and that appropriate action would be taken with respect to differences.

(b) Benefits to Nonprofit Organizations

Internal accounting control provides important benefits to nonprofit organizations. It improves the quality of information and reduces the possibility of:

- error,
- mismanagement, and
- fraud.

This in turn increases the probability that the organization will be able to provide effective service to the community, and also reduces the possibility that (1) an organization will incur a loss of public trust, and (2) its board and management will suffer public censure or legal penalties.

(c) Internal Accounting Controls Are Not Static

Nonprofit organizations and the environments in which they operate are dynamic. Internal accounting controls must change in response to the changing character of an organization and its environment, and the changing relationship between the two. Existing controls may become redundant, irrelevant, or cost inefficient and need to be eliminated. New controls may become necessary. *Periodic review is essential to maintaining the vitality of internal control systems.*

(d) Role of the Board of Directors and Senior Management

The board of directors and senior management have ultimate responsibility for internal accounting control. This responsibility is particularly pronounced in nonprofit organizations, where scarce resources often limit the extent and effectiveness of formal control systems. Internal accounting control in nonprofit organizations is improved by the continuous monitoring of accounting records and procedures, and the overall review of operations by directors and senior management.

23A.2 ELEMENTS OF AN EFFECTIVE INTERNAL ACCOUNTING CONTROL SYSTEM

Effective internal accounting control is achieved through an integrated system of people, records, and procedures. The key elements of an effective system are:

- control environment
- director and management involvement
- control objectives
- organization structure and management controls
- key policies and procedures manuals
- segregation of duties
- recordkeeping and information system
- financial reporting system
- budgets
- periodic review of the control system
- cost-benefit analysis

(a) Control Environment

Program and administrative staff must understand the importance and philosophy of internal accounting control before an effective system can be initiated. If a control system does not reflect control requirements, or if control procedures are improperly executed, effective management may be impossible and the goals of the organization may not be realized.

Creating a control environment is often an educational process best performed by senior management. Not only must management inspire commitment to control, it must ensure that the personnel complement of the organization is of sufficient size, competence, and discipline to execute control functions. It must be clear from the attitude and posture of directors and management that effective controls are a matter of high priority.

(b) Director and Management Involvement

Control systems are more effective if directors and management who authorize programs and execute transactions are involved in the day-to-day management of the organization. In many instances, the chairman of the board or finance committee chairman will be a business executive who can effectively monitor a control system and determine whether it is operating satisfactorily.

Senior management can also play a vital role in the control process by expressing interest in the day-to-day accounting and financial routines, through inquiries and observation. A well-phrased question from time to time can be a more effective control technique than merely a structured set of formal procedures.

(c) Control Objectives

Overall internal accounting control objectives should be established for the organization, as well as for each individual area of operation. Internal accounting control objectives generally include control over authorization of transactions, recording of transactions, access to assets, and asset accountability. Internal accounting controls should reflect the unique environment, attributes, and risks inherent in the operation of each organization. Key control objectives for each major area of operation should be identified and set forth in written procedures.

(d) Organization Structure and Management Controls

Organization structure and management controls should facilitate establishment of control objectives and execution of control procedures.

Organization structure should contain the following attributes:

- clear lines of authority
- clear definition of responsibility
- authority commensurate with responsibilities

Organization structure and management controls should address, when necessary, problems associated with use of volunteer personnel.

(e) Key Policies and Procedures Manuals

The operating policies of an organization and the accounting procedures for executing transactions should be clearly communicated. These policies and procedures should be readily accessible to appropriate personnel, and should serve as the primary source of reference for resolving operating and accounting questions. Effective communication is often achieved by collecting and codifying policies and procedures in reference manuals, particularly when part-time and volunteer personnel control certain aspects of operations.

(f) Segregation of Duties

Responsibilities should be assigned to personnel in such a manner that no one individual, including senior managers and directors, controls all aspects of processing a transaction.

Segregation of duties is a coordinated system of checks and balances in which tasks necessary to complete a transaction either are performed by different individuals, or two or more individuals working in tandem, or are independently reviewed. Division of work assignments along these lines reduces the probability that error, mismanagement, or fraud will go undetected.

Segregation of duties is the cornerstone of internal accounting control. It is often expensive to implement and expected costs and benefits should be carefully analyzed before a decision to enhance or implement is made. Nonprofit organizations often do not have sufficient personnel to achieve a traditional segregation of duties. In such instances, active involvement of directors and senior management in monitoring the course of activities and the flow of resources into and out of an organization is essential.

(g) Recordkeeping and Information Systems

Information is a key component of a system of internal accounting control. Accurate and timely information permits an organization to examine and verify past transactions and current levels of assets. Collection, classification, and accumulation of information is, therefore, essential to an effective system of internal accounting control.

Collection of information is generally initiated by the person or persons executing the transaction.

Classification of information is achieved by virtue of a chart of accounts. A chart of accounts is a collection of codes which classify transactions on the basis of type of transaction and responsibility for the transaction.

Accumulation of information is generally accomplished through summary or subsidiary journals and a general ledger. Subsidiary journals summarize records of similar transactions and are, in turn, summarized in the general ledger. A hierarchy of accounting records and segregation of responsibility for each are important elements of internal accounting control.

The following records generally provide information necessary for internal accounting control in nonprofit organizations:

- cash receipts journal
- cash disbursements journal
- accounts receivable ledger
- accounts payable register
- payroll register
- fixed asset ledger
- investment ledger
- general journal
- general ledger

Electronic data processing. Many nonprofit organizations use electronic data processing (EDP) to perform routine administrative functions and to manage information. While EDP management controls and control techniques differ from manual control procedures, control objectives for EDP systems are similar to those of any processing system.

The transition from manual to EDP systems often creates new areas of control exposure which must be promptly addressed.

Service bureaus. Many nonprofit organizations engage outside organizations, known as service bureaus, to prepare payrolls and vendor checks, and to maintain selected financial records. Use of service bureaus, like use of EDP, does not change the objectives of internal accounting control or the control responsibilities of directors and management. New control procedures applicable to both the nonprofit organization and the service bureau are, however, often required.

A thorough understanding of control procedures surrounding the processing of transactions at service bureaus is essential. A well-defined system of input and output controls is often necessary to provide control over service bureau activities.

(h) Financial Reporting System

A concise, comprehensible and timely report detailing the financial activity of each major area of operation should be prepared. Such reports provide assurance concerning the propriety and accuracy of reported transactions. Since nonprofit personnel may not be conversant with technical accounting conventions, functional financial reporting will be an effective control only to the extent it is simple and straightforward. Effective financial reports often contain the following attributes:

- highlights of important transactions and trends
- written analysis of operations
- nontechnical terminology
- concise display of information
- comparison of actual results to expected results

(i) Budgets

Budgets are an important element of an internal accounting control system. They allow effective monitoring of the flow of resources in and out of an organization. In nonprofit organizations, comparison of actual results to budget estimates often provides the first indication of operating problems or weaknesses in an internal accounting control system.

Three types of budgets are generally prepared:

- operating budget

- cash flow budget
- capital budget

Operating budgets project revenue and expenditures for one or more future periods. Forecasts are based on historical events and current assumptions concerning the future.

Cash flow budgets estimate cash receipts and cash disbursements. They forecast cash balances at different intervals in the operating cycle.

Capital budgets specify future expenditures on capital acquisitions—land, buildings, and equipment—which have been formally authorized by the board. Normally, only capital expenditures approved by this budget are permitted during the period.

Internal accounting control is facilitated by preparation of:

- periodic budgets
- comparative financial information

Periodic budgets are the division of annual budgets into quarterly or monthly segments. Periodic budgets should reflect seasonal variations in income, expenditures, cash flow, and fixed asset purchases.

Comparative financial information includes actual income, expenditures, cash flow, and fixed asset purchases for the current period and comparable data from preceding periods.

Material variances from periodic budgets and between current and prior periods should be promptly investigated and satisfactory explanations obtained by the chief financial officer.

(j) Periodic Review of the Control System

Control procedures which are currently effective may become ineffectual if the nature of an organization, its activities, or types of transactions change. Periodic review of the control system assures that control procedures in need of change are identified on a timely basis. Questions which facilitate control system review include the following:

- Have changes occurred in our organization which may require new controls?

- Have "surprises" been encountered which could have been anticipated with better controls?
- Have explanations of variations from budget been confusing or contradictory?
- Have our accounting or financial functions been overextended, increasing the possibility of error or untimely processing of transactions?
- Have recommendations for improving our control system made by independent accountants been implemented?

(k) Cost-Benefit Analysis

Every organization should have formal procedures for determining whether recommendations for improving the control system are cost-justified. Cost-benefit analysis is an effective method of analyzing control recommendations.

Cost-benefit or risk analysis examines the cost of new control procedures in the context of the benefits to be derived from eliminating a control weakness. In other words, it compares the likely cost-saving which would accompany reduction of risk with the out-of-pocket expense (and intangible costs) of risk reduction. Cost-benefit analysis should be conducted subsequent to discovery of an internal control weakness or introduction of a new type of transaction, but prior to implementing new control procedures.

The following sequence is useful in applying cost-benefit analysis to internal accounting controls:

- Identify the internal accounting control weakness.
- Determine the importance of the weakness with respect to:

  —magnitude of possible risk

  —probable frequency of occurrence
- Identify controls which could be implemented.
- Identify cost elements, both quantitative and qualitative. Costs frequently include:

  —direct expenditure on controls

ponse to new restrictions

nts, both quantitative and qualitative. ide:

loss of resources

e

e or priority ranking to cost and benefit nates and judgments are often required.

lysis and document premises upon which a

ed if total benefits derived exceed the total ontrol procedures are available, the control nefits should be selected.

benefit analysis is incremental costs and ar expended on controls should produce at nefits.

23A.3 BASIC INTERNAL ACCOUNTING CONTROL SYSTEM

The following section sets forth a framework for a basic internal accounting control system surrounding cash receipts, cash disbursements, payrolls, receivables, payables, inventory, fixed assets, and petty cash and other working funds. In each control area, *control objectives* and *control procedures* are identified. Control objectives define goals pertaining to each control area. Control procedures identify controls related to each area. Alternate procedures can often be used to achieve control objectives; those suggested in this section are commonly found in nonprofit organizations.

Control procedures are presented as questions to assist directors and managers to assess present controls. "No" answers signal control weaknesses which should be evaluated in terms of magnitude and mitigating circumstances, such as compensating controls.

(a) Receipt of cash

Control objective: To ensure that all cash intended for the organization is received, promptly deposited, properly recorded, reconciled, and kept under adequate security.

Control procedures:

Are the cash receiving, processing, recording, and bank reconciliation functions clearly segregated?

Is cash listed and are checks restrictively endorsed immediately upon receipt?

Are prenumbered receipts issued? Is adequate control maintained over the sequence of unused and used numbers?

Is the initial listing of receipts sent directly to persons responsible for the general ledger and bank reconciliation functions?

Does a duplicate listing of receipts accompany receipts for use in preparing deposits and posting detail receivable records?

Is cash deposited in a bank account intact, and on a timely basis, by a person independent of receiving and general ledger functions? Are duplicate deposit slips received?

Alternatively, is cash received directly by a bank, which authenticates and forwards deposit slips and a list of depositors and deposits to the organization?

Is the initial listing of receipts compared with duplicate bank deposit slips? Is a receipts summary prepared by the receipts processing function for use in posting the cash receipts journal?

Is the cash receipts journal posted by a person independent of the receiving and cash processing functions?

Is the cash receipts journal posted to the general ledger by a person independent of the cash receiving and processing functions?

Are bank reconciliations prepared by a person independent of the cash receiving, processing and recording functions?

(b) Disbursement of Cash

Control objective: To ensure that cash is disbursed only upon proper authorization of management, for valid business purposes, and that all disbursements are properly recorded.

Control procedures:

Are the authorization, processing, check signing, recording, and bank reconciliation functions clearly segregated?

Are persons authorized to approve expenditures clearly identified, and are all expenditures approved in advance by authorized persons?

Are invoices or requests for expense reimbursements supported by appropriate receipts and/or approval indicating receipt of goods or services? Is this policy effectively communicated to all appropriate persons, including volunteers?

Are all disbursements made by prenumbered checks?

Is a record of cash disbursements (e.g., check stubs, check copies, cash disbursements record) kept by person processing checks? Does a listing of disbursement amounts accompany the checks for signature?

Is check-signing authority vested in persons at appropriately high levels in the organization? Do larger checks require a higher level of authority? Is the number of authorized signatures limited to the minimum practical number?

Are signed checks mailed promptly under the control of the check-signer?

Does the checksigner (1) review and initial documentation supporting checks indicating completeness and appropriate approval and (2) compare check amounts, on a test basis, to the listing of disbursements accompanying checks?

Is the listing of disbursements initialled by the checksigner and compared to the disbursement summary prepared by the check processing function for use in posting the cash disbursement journal by a person independent of the check processing, checksigning, and authorization functions?

Is the cash disbursements journal posted by a person independent of the authorization, check processing and checksigning functions?

Is the cash disbursements journal posted to the general ledger by a person independent of the check processing, checksigning, and authorization functions?

Are bank statements and canceled checks received directly and reconciled with disbursement records by a person independent of the cash authorization, check processing, and checksigning functions?

(c) Payroll

Control objective: To ensure that payroll disbursements are made only upon proper authorization of management to bona fide employees, that payroll disbursements are properly recorded, and that related legal requirements (such as payroll tax deposits) are complied with.

Control procedures:

Are the personnel authorization, payroll preparation and approval, payroll check distribution, recordkeeping, and bank reconciliation functions clearly segregated?

Are changes in employment (additions and terminations), salaries, wage rates, and payroll deductions authorized by proper nonaccounting personnel? Do policies and procedures exist for accounting for vacations, holidays, and sick leave?

Are changes in employment status recorded in employee personnel files which are maintained by a person independent of the payroll processing function?

Are time and attendance records, including hours worked, overtime, and special benefits, reviewed and approved by authorized nonaccounting personnel?

Is the payroll register kept by person(s) processing payroll checks? Does the register accompany the checks for signature?

Is a separate imprest basis payroll bank account maintained? Is this account periodically reconciled? Is a maximum dollar amount set which can be drawn on this account?

Are all disbursements made by prenumbered checks?

Is checksigning authority consistent with that for general disbursements?

Are signed checks distributed promptly under the control of the checksigner?

Are payroll registers reviewed and initialled by the checksigner? Does the review periodically include, on a test basis:

- Comparison of current and previous payrolls?
- Comparison of check amounts with payroll register?
- Comparison of changes in wage rates with personnel department records?
- Comparison of hours worked with time records?
- Verifying accuracy of payroll computations?

Is the payroll register initialled by the checksigner compared to the payroll summary prepared by the payroll processing function for use in posting the general ledger?

Is the summary of the payroll register posted to the general ledger by a person independent of the payroll processing, checksigning, and authorization functions?

Are bank statements and canceled checks received directly and reconciled with the payroll register by a person independent of the payroll processing, checksigning and authorization functions?

Are unclaimed payroll checks controlled by an individual not involved in payroll processing, checksigning, or distribution functions?

Are the mailing of W-2 forms and the investigation of questions arising therefrom the responsibility of individuals independent of the authorization, payroll processing, and checksigning functions?

Is payroll classified in proper accounts (e.g., by function) and is classification periodically reviewed?

Are the information supplied to employee benefit plans, and actuarial assumptions and computations periodically reviewed?

Are the taxes (e.g., social security and unemployment) paid on the wages of each employee monitored? Are all such taxes paid when due?

(d) Billing and Receivables

Control objective: To ensure that all sales or services are promptly billed and recorded at authorized rates, that payments are received promptly and unpaid accounts adequately followed up.

Control procedures:

Are the credit authorization, billing, recordkeeping, collection, and cash processing functions clearly segregated?

Are all billings for services or goods approved in advance by authorized persons?

Are authorized rates for services and prices for goods clearly established and effectively communicated to those responsible for the billing function? Are changes in rates or prices promptly communicated?

Are billings promptly recorded in receivable records or are copies of billings maintained in distinct open invoice files? Are control totals of billings prepared by the billing function daily and promptly forwarded to the general ledger function?

Are accounts receivable records protected from theft, destruction and alteration?

Is the accounts receivable ledger or open invoice file periodically reconciled with the general ledger by a person independent of the billing and receivable records and initial receipt of cash functions?

Payment—see Receipt of cash (subsection (a)).

Are collections promptly recorded in receivable records or on copies of billings by a person independent of the initial receipt of cash?

Are all adjustments to original billings approved by nonaccounting persons?

Is the prompt collection of outstanding accounts initiated? Are statements of account periodically sent to persons with outstanding accounts?

Are disputed accounts reviewed by an authorized person who is independent of the billing and receivable records function?

Are accounts outstanding properly analyzed for collectibility and periodically aged by a person independent of the billing and receivable functions?

Is the write-off of uncollectible amounts approved by nonaccounting persons?

(e) Accounts Payable

Control objective: To ensure that accounts payable are supported by appropriate documentation, are promptly paid and properly recorded. See also Disbursement of cash (subsection (b)).

Control procedures:

Are the authorization, processing, recording and payment functions clearly segregated?

Authorization—see Disbursement of cash (subsection (b)).

Are all approved invoices promptly recorded in the voucher (accounts payable) register to establish control for payment?

Are unpaid invoices maintained in a distinct unpaid open invoice file?

Are statements from vendors regularly compared with open invoice files?

Are invoices from unfamiliar or unusual vendors reviewed and approved for payment by authorized personnel who are independent of the invoice processing function?

Payment—see Disbursement of cash (subsection (b)).

Are payments promptly recorded in the accounts payable register to avoid double payment?

Is the accounts payable register periodically reconciled with the general ledger by a person independent of the invoice processing function?

Is a listing of unpaid invoices regularly prepared and periodically reconciled with the general ledger by a person independent of the invoice processing function?

(f) Inventory

Control objective: To ensure that inventory is appropriately safeguarded and properly recorded.

Control procedures:

Are the purchasing, custodial, processing, and recordkeeping functions clearly segregated?

Is responsibility for inventory established and appropriate physical safeguards maintained?

Is the receipt, transfer, and withdrawal of inventory items promptly recorded in inventory records, and are quantity records of the more important inventory items maintained?

Are inventory records periodically reconciled with the general ledger?

Is a physical inventory periodically taken by persons independent of custody and processing functions?

Do inventory records permit accounting for items that are expensed when purchased?

(g) Fixed assets

Control objective: To ensure that fixed assets are acquired and disposed of only upon proper authorization, are adequately safeguarded, and properly recorded.

Control procedures:

Are the authorization, purchasing, custody, and recordkeeping functions clearly segregated?

Are only fixed asset purchases approved by the board in the capital budget permitted? Is a board-approved amended capital budget required for purchases not initially authorized?

Is borrowing for fixed asset purchases limited to specific authorizations by the board in the capital budget?

Do requests for capital additions include identification of assets being replaced, and the likely disposition of the replaced asset?

Is the sale, retirement or abandonment of fixed assets in conformity with board policy, and subject to approval by the board?

Is the fixed asset ledger periodically reconciled with the general ledger by a person independent of the recording and custody functions?

Are independent appraisals of fixed assets for insurance purposes periodically made?

Are land, buildings, and equipment recorded in a fixed asset ledger? Do asset records include description, location, identification number, date of acquisition, and cost of each asset?

Are fully depreciated fixed assets and fixed assets not currently in use recorded in the fixed asset ledger?

Have criteria been established by the board for capitalizing or expensing fixed asset purchases?

Have depreciation policies been established by the board?

Are custodial accountability and physical safeguards maintained by each unit of the organization which has the responsibility for fixed assets?

Is the movement of equipment from one department to another reported to the recording function promptly?

Are physical inventories of fixed assets periodically taken by persons independent of custody and recording functions?

(h) Petty Cash and Other Working Funds

Control objective: To ensure that petty cash and other working funds are disbursed only for proper purposes, are adequately safeguarded, and properly recorded.

Control procedures:

Are petty cash and other working funds maintained on an imprest basis?

Is the responsibility for each fund vested in a single custodian?

Are the types and amounts of petty cash disbursements limited?

Are advances to employees from the petty cash fund authorized by appropriate personnel?

Are petty cash transactions periodically monitored, and are increased levels of activity investigated?

Do persons receiving cash sign petty cash vouchers? Are amounts written in letters and numbers?

Are petty cash reimbursement checks payable only to the custodian? Once the fund is reimbursed, are vouchers and receipts marked to prevent reuse?

Are surprise counts of petty cash funds made by an individual other than the custodian?

Are physical safeguards over petty cash funds, including fire-resistant boxes, vaults, and overnight depositories, maintained?

23A.4 SPECIFIC NONPROFIT INTERNAL ACCOUNTING CONTROLS

Each nonprofit organization has aspects of its operations which require specific control consideration. This section contains a series of control questions relating to several types of transactions frequently executed by nonprofit organizations, which will assist directors and managers to assess the effectiveness of controls presently surrounding these transactions. Again, "no" answers signal control weaknesses which should be evaluated in terms of magnitude and mitigating circumstances, such as compensating controls.

(a) Tuition

Control objective: To ensure that all tuition due is promptly collected at authorized rates and properly recorded.

Control procedures:

Is the receipt and recording of tuition payments segregated from the tuition receivable function?

Is tuition remitted by check, payable only to the institution?

Is tuition due at, or prior to, registration, or early in the period the course is given? If payment is due serially, are payments according to an installment plan schedule?

Are tuition receipts periodically compared with the tuition revenue estimates in the operating budget?

Is tuition revenue periodically compared with enrollment data from nonaccounting departments, such as the registrar's or recorder's office?

Are tuition adjustments, allowances, and credits approved by an authorized nonaccounting official? Is the write-off of tuition receivables limited to authorized nonaccounting personnel?

If tuition is based on a standard charge (per semester, for example), is the amount paid by each student compared with the standard, by an individucal independent of billing, cash receipt and recording functions?

If tuition is based on the number or type of courses (or credit hours), is enrollment data for each student verified with registration data from nonaccounting departments, and is arithmetic computation of tuition checked by an individual independent of the billing, cash receipt and recording functions?

Are tuition receivables periodically reviewed to determine whether they have been properly analyzed for collectibility and are properly aged, by a person independent of the recording and receivable function?

Are current delinquents (past due less than one semester) actively pursued and are long-term delinquencies turned over to a collection agency?

Is the enrollment, awarding of degrees, and providing of transcripts to delinquent students prohibited?

(b) Membership Dues

Control objective: To ensure that all membership dues are promptly collected in authorized amounts and properly recorded.

Control procedures:

Are the receipt and recording of dues payments segregated from the dues receivable function?

Are dues paid by check, payable only to the organization?

Are dues paid prior to, or at the beginning of, the membership period? If payment is due serially, are payments according to an installment plan schedule?

If the amount of dues paid is based on the size of a member organization:

- Is organization membership verified with nonaccounting records, such as industry surveys?
- Are organization dues periodically compared with the graduated dues schedule?
- Is the arithmetic computation of organization dues checked?

Are dues receipts periodically compared with dues revenue estimates in the operating budget?

Are dues receipts periodically compared with membership data from nonaccounting departments?

Is dues payment information promptly forwarded from accounting to the membership department?

Are persons receiving services, as indicated by mailing lists for periodicals, attendance lists for seminars and enrollment in insurance plans, periodically compared with persons paying dues?

Are dues receivable periodically reviewed to determine whether receivables are properly analyzed for collectibility and are properly aged, by a person independent of the recording and receivable function?

Is the write-off of dues receivable limited to authorized nonaccounting personnel?

Is the granting of memberships in future periods to delinquent members prohibited?

(c) Contributions

Control objective: To ensure that substantially all contributions intended for the organization are received, promptly deposited and properly recorded.

Control procedures: An excellent discussion of internal accounting control of contributions is contained in *Audits of Voluntary Health and Welfare Organizations* issued by the AICPA.

- *Direct mail*

Internal accounting control of incoming mail is similar to controls discussed for Receipt of cash (subsection (a)).

- *Direct solicitation*

Is an organization pyramid established with each level responsible to the next higher level?

Is the distribution of authorized solicitation material strictly limited?

Are collections deposited at the lowest possible level?

Is accounting control separated from the physical control of cash at the earliest possible point?

Are reports prepared which account for all areas and all solicitors?

- *Radio and television solicitation*

Are pledges promptly recorded and is collection promptly instituted?
Are receipt, recording and custody of collections segregated?

- *Contributions from uncontrolled organizations (e.g., United Way)*

Are amounts due the organization periodically reviewed to determine whether proper amounts are received?

- *Special events*

Accounting control of special events is similar to control of ticket revenue (see subsection (h)).

(d) Grants, Gifts, and Bequests Received

Control objective: To ensure that all grants, gifts, and bequests are received and properly recorded, and that compliance with the terms of any related restrictions is adequately monitored.

Control procedures:

Is the receipt and recording of grants, gifts, and bequests segregated from expenditure and monitoring of amounts expended?

Once notified of grant, gift, or bequest award, is the amount expected to be received recorded in a separate receivable account?

If award is not received on a timely basis, is the awarding party promptly notified? If the write-off of a grant, gift, or bequest receivable is necessary, is the write-off approved by authorized nonaccounting personnel?

Once the award is received, is the amount received recorded by an individual who is independent of the cash receipts function?

Are differences between expected and actual awards promptly investigated?

Are awards contingent upon future events periodically monitored?

If possible, are budget estimates prepared for grants, gifts and bequests? Are award receipts periodically compared with award estimates in the operating budget?

If an organization is responsible for funds used by an individual associated with the organization, does the organization maintain accounts independent of accounts kept by the recipient?

- Is the disbursement of funds to award recipients approved by nonaccounting personnel?
- Are restrictions on use of awards documented? Is compliance with restrictions verified before the initial and all subsequent disbursements?
- In the case of grants, are accounts periodically monitored for unexpended funds, and are they promptly returned to the awarding party, if necessary?

(i) Grants Awarded to Others

Control objective: To ensure that grants are awarded and paid to others only upon proper authorization, and are properly recorded, and that grantee compliance with the grant terms is adequately monitored.

Control procedures:

Are the review and approval, disbursement, recording, and monitoring functions clearly segregated?

Does the grant application identify eligible applicants and projects?

Is each payment of a grant award authorized by the board or appropriate nonaccounting personnel?

Is the grantee promptly notified of the award and the conditions of the award, and is grantee acceptance in writing required?

Once awarded, are grants promptly recorded as a grant payable?

Does an individual independent of the authorization and disbursement functions verify that payments are made to proper recipients in correct amounts, and that payment is triggered by an appropriate event?

Do recipients file periodic reports documenting use of grants, which are reviewed by nonaccounting personnel?

For grants payable from endowment or other trust funds:

- Does the disbursement policy define status of investment principal with respect to preservation or erosion?
- Are cash levels continuously monitored to determine whether scheduled payments can be made without eroding principal?
- Is the level of income and disbursements periodically monitored to determine whether disbursements conform to percentage or other distribution policy of the board?

(f) Loans

Control objective: To ensure that loan funds are properly recorded, disbursed only to authorized persons, and repaid when due.

Control procedures:

Are the authorization, disbursement, custody, recording, and collection functions clearly segregated?

Are new loan funds classified and recorded in separate accounts on the basis of restrictions and sources?

- Types of restrictions include student need, domicile of student, course of study, etc.
- Types of sources include federally funded programs, board-designated unrestricted funds, endowment and other gifts, etc.

If provision of loan funds to the institution is contingent upon matching or percentage contributions by the institution, is the extent and computation of the institution's commitment verified?

If endowment is received with the stipulation that investment income (or part thereof) is to be used for loans, is investment income periodically reviewed to determine whether it is received on a timely basis, in appropriate amounts, and is recorded in the proper loan fund account?

If possible, are budget estimates prepared for loan funds? Are loan receipts periodically compared with loan estimates in the operating budget?

Are the different types of loan programs, including scholarships, fellowships, grants-in-aid, and part-time employment, fully documented and periodically reviewed for revisions?

Are disbursements periodically reviewed to determine whether they are in conformity with the financial assistance policies of the institution, and in compliance with restrictions on loan funds and programs?

- Accounting and financial aid records are reviewed to determine the amount of loans students have previously received, the amount of loans students are currently eligible to receive, etc.
- Student personnel and financial aid records are reviewed to verify whether students qualify for loans on such bases as need, citizenship, enrollment status, etc.

Are loan fund assets, usually cash, notes receivable, and short-term investments, periodically reviewed to determine whether the loan fund balance is consistent with executing the loan policy of the organization?

Are loan disbursement records periodically reviewed to determine whether loan funds are used only for designated purposes, and not such undesignated purposes as current operations?

Is repayment by check, payable to the organization?

Are loan receivables periodically reviewed to determine whether receivables are properly analyzed for collectibility and are properly aged, by a person independent of the loan recording and receivable function?

Is the computation of principal and interest repayment checked for accuracy?

Are delinquent loan procedures reviewed to determine whether they comply with the requirements of different loan programs? (Federal agencies establish loan retrieval guidelines for federally funded programs.)

Additional questions related to accounting controls for delinquent loans include:

- Is a deadline established after which unpaid loans are in default?
- Are delinquent loans promptly turned over to a collection agency?

- Are loans which are forgiven periodically reviewed to determine whether cancellations are properly authorized and are in conformity with loan policy?
- Are loan delinquents prohibited from receiving new loans?
- Is the write-off of loan receivables limited to authorized nonaccounting personnel?

(g) Endowments and Investment Income

Control objective: To ensure that endowment assets are properly recorded, adequately safeguarded, and managed in accordance with any related restrictions and prudent investment management practices, and that all investment income due is promptly collected and deposited and properly recorded.

Control procedures:

Are the receipt, recording, custody, transaction authorization and performance monitoring functions clearly segregated?

Are endowments recorded in separate accounts, and are restrictions on investment principal and investment income documented?

Are endowments recorded in the investment ledger by a person independent of initial receipt or custody of endowment securities?

Is the investment ledger reconciled with the general ledger by a person independent of the initial receipt, custody or recording of endowment securities?

Are endowment securities deposited with an independent custodian or in a bank safe deposit box?

- If deposited with an independent custodian, are accounting and custodial functions segregated? Does the custodian issue periodic reports to the organization? Does the custodian carry sufficient fidelity insurance?
- If deposited in a bank safe deposit box, is access limited to two or more authorized persons, and are all visits recorded?

Are investment securities in the name of the organization, or an appropriate "street" name?

Are security transactions, including purchases, sales, renewals, and exchanges, approved by authorized nonaccounting personnel (usually the investment committee of the board or an appropriate financial officer)?

Is the basis of valuation of investment securities periodically reviewed?

Is the write-down and write-off of endowment securities limited to authorized nonaccounting personnel?

Is the disbursement of restricted investment income reviewed by appropriate nonaccounting personnel to determine whether the disbursement is in conformity with donor or board-imposed restrictions? Are restrictions on and proposed uses of investment income reviewed prior to disbursement?

Is investment income received periodically compared with investment revenue estimates in the operating budget?

Are the promptness and accuracy of investment income payments by underlying companies and investment counselors reviewed?

If securities are "pooled" for investment purposes, are the allocation formula and the computation and distribution of investment income and realized and unrealized gains and losses periodically reviewed? Are investment income and realized and unrealized gains distinguished?

(h) Other Nonprofit Internal Accounting Controls

Is the pledge billing and receivable function segregated from the cash receipt function?

Are pledges promptly recorded, and is collection promptly initiated?

Is the aging and collectibility of pledges, as well as the allowance for uncollectible pledges, periodically reviewed?

Are collection policy and experience, age of pledges, current economic conditions, and credit standing of pledgor, examined when reporting pledge income?

Once received, are pledges recorded in separate accounts and are restrictions documented?

Are pledge receipts periodically compared with pledge estimates in the operating budget?

Internal accounting control of donated fixed assets and donated investments is similar to control of purchased fixed assets (subsection (g)) and endowment securities, respectively.

Internal accounting control of donated materials is similar to control of inventory. The basis of valuation is periodically reviewed, and, if donated materials are significant, a comparison to budget estimates is made.

Internal accounting control of donated services addresses the following issues:

- Is valuation for each position compared with the fair value of the service contributed?
- Are time records periodically reviewed to determine whether services are performed?
- Is the nature of contributed services periodically reviewed to determine whether the services are appropriate for the organization?
- If material, are budget estimates prepared for donated services? Are actual donated services periodically compared with donated services estimates in the operating budget?

Are agency funds segregated from other funds, and separately accounted for and reported on?

Is disbursement contingent upon written authorization of the owning individual or organization?

Are the ticket issuance and cash receipts functions segregated from the recording of ticket sales?

Is ticket printing and inventory periodically reviewed, and are records of tickets printed, issued, used and unused, kept?

Are ticket sales records maintained, and is ticket revenue periodically compared to ticket sales?

Is ticket revenue periodically compared to the ticket revenue estimates in the operating budget?

CHAPTER 25

Investments

25.2 CALCULATING SHARE VALUES IN POOLED INVESTMENTS

(a) Cost Basis Accounting

p. 436. *Add at end of note 1:*

See the discussion, in Chapter 8 of this supplement, of the FASB statement on accounting for marketable securities. Briefly, it requires such investments to be reported at current fair market value.

PART FIVE

Tax and Compliance Reporting Requirements

CHAPTER 29

Audits of Federally-Funded Programs

29.1 BASIC REQUIREMENTS

p. 533. ***In Exhibit 29–1, within Notes * and **, change 29.4 to:***
29.5.

p. 533. ***Add to note 2:***

As of late 1995, the OMB had proposed raising the threshold at which an audit is required to $300,000.

29.2 REQUIREMENTS AND DEFINITIONS

(b) Major and Nonmajor Programs

p. 537. ***Add at end of subsection:***
In 1995, the OMB proposed changes in this definition designed to have auditors focus more attention on programs that are most at risk of having problems, not simply on the larger programs.

29.4 WHAT TO EXPECT FROM THE AUDIT

(b) What Will Be Included in the Report?

p. 545. *Add at end of subsection:*
In 1995, the OMB proposed to shorten the filing deadline to nine months. This change has not yet become effective.

29.5 STEPS BEING TAKEN TO IMPROVE THE PROCESS

p. 546. *Add at end of section:*
In early 1995, the Office of Management and Budget issued several proposed changes to Circular A-133. If adopted, they will change the thresholds at which an audit is required, the filing deadline, the definition of major program, and the forms of some of the auditor's reports, and simplify the audit reporting process when no problems are discovered. As of late 1995, neither the timing nor the exact form of the final version of these changes can be predicted.

PART SIX

Setting Up and Keeping the Books

CHAPTER 31

Simplified Accrual Basis Bookkeeping

31.3 MONTHLY ACCRUAL ENTRIES

p. 572. ***Add to numbered list:***

7. An entry to adjust the value of marketable securities to current market value.

p. 577. ***Add new subsection at end of section:***

(h) Adjustment of Marketable Securities to Current Market Value (New)

Organizations that own marketable securities covered by the new FASB standard, discussed in Chapter 8 of this supplement, will have to adjust the recorded value up or down each period as the value of the investments fluctuates with the securities markets. Note that this entry is required whether or not any investments were actually disposed of during the period. The entry to record an increase in value is:

July 31

Entry No. 6

Debit No. 5 Marketable securities ....$ 2,745

Credit No. 57 Gain or loss on sale of assets ....$ 2,745

To record increase in market value of investments during the month of July.

As discussed in Sections 8.1(d)–(f), the gain is reported in the unrestricted class of net assets, regardless of whether the investments relate to an unrestricted or restricted fund, unless the gain is considered to be legally restricted because of an explicit donor stipulation, or provisions of applicable state law.

If the investments had declined in value, the entry would be reversed:

July 31

Entry No. 7

Debit No. 57 Gain or loss on sale of securities ....$ 2,745

Credit No. 5 Marketable securities ....$ 2,745

To record decrease in market value of investments during the month of July.

CHAPTER 32

Full Accrual Basis Bookkeeping

32.8 MONTHLY ACCRUAL ENTRIES

p. 603. ***Add new subsection at end of section:***

(g) Investments (New)

An entry must be made to adjust the value of marketable securities to current market value. This entry is discussed in Section 31.3 in this supplement.

APPENDIX D (NEW)

Exposure Draft of New AICPA Audit and Accounting Guide: Not-for-Profit Organizations

In April 1995, the AICPA issued an exposure draft of a proposed new audit and accounting guide for not-for-profit organizations. Its principal provisions—those that do not merely repeat other literature—are listed here. The exact timing of issuance of the final guide cannot be predicted, but it is not likely to be before the spring of 1996, at the earliest.

Exposure period: Until August 14, 1995 (120 days from release of draft). The guide explicitly incorporates provisions of SFAS Nos. 116 and 117, and SOP 94-2 and 94-3.

Page or paragraph references in this appendix are to the first time a matter is discussed.

EXHIBIT—SPECIFIC ISSUES FOR COMMENT (page v)

- Guide refers to pars. 53 and 54 of SFAS No. 116 regarding pass-through gifts, and seeks input on certain specific situations involving limited discretion on the part of the initial recipient as to the ultimate destination of such gifts.
- Guide is silent about treatment of certain college tuition discounts, and seeks input on the issue.

PREFACE

- Applicability/scope: nongovernmental not-for-profits (NFPs); aspects of GAAP and GAAS that are unique or particularly significant (p. xv).
- Supersedes existing guides: Voluntary Health & Welfare; Colleges (including SOP 74-8); Other Not-for-Profits (including SOP 78-10) (p. xvi).
- Effective date: Periods beginning after June 15, 1995, except for small (total assets less than $5 million and annual expenses less than $1 million) organizations, for which the date is December 15, 1995. Early application is permitted (p. xvi). [This will change.]
- Adoption: Choice of retroactive or prospective (pp. xvi-xvii).

Number references from this point on are to paragraphs in the draft.

CHAPTER 1—INTRODUCTION

- Scope: not-for-profit organizations as defined in SFAS No. 117 (par. 1.01); lists all types covered by existing audit guides/SOPs.

  —Some NFPs do not meet SFAS No. 117 definition, but are required to follow this guide (e.g., country clubs), except that for matters where guide conflicts with other FASB rules applicable to for-profits from which NFPs are exempt (e.g., SFAS No. 115), those organizations must follow FASB for-profit rules (1.04 & footnote 2).

  —Does not cover NFP entities for which there are other audit guides: pension plans, mutual insurance, credit unions, CIRAs, health care (unless a voluntary health and welfare organization) (1.05).
- Discusses GAAP hierarchy (1.06–1.07).

CHAPTER 2—GENERAL AUDITING

For planning, auditor should consider:

- Legal restrictions imposed by donors, contracts, the organization's governing board, and others, including tax laws (2.07–2.08).
- Audit risk, especially associated with receiving contributions (2.09).
- Unique reporting requirements: expenses by function, SFAS No. 116 disclosures (2.11).
- Management responses to environmental pressures unique to NFPs (2.13):

  —Attempt to manage revenue to maximize donations based on revenues.

  —Reduced contributions may cause management to pursue overly aggressive investment strategies.

  —Adverse demographics may lead to aggressive marketing of fee-based services and poor collectibility of receivables.

  —Reduced unrestricted gifts may lead to improper use of restricted resources.

  —Obligation to comply with requirements of federal grants.

  —Attempt to misallocate expenses between program and supporting services.
- Aspects of internal control environment unique to NFPs (2.18).
- Examples of specific analytical review procedures unique to NFPs (2.21):

  —Industry data on endowment returns, contributions, operating costs.

  —Student enrollment and tuition revenue, members and dues revenue, stagehand costs and number of performances.
- Refers to guidance on compliance auditing in Yellow Book, A-133, SOP 92-9, SAS 74 (2.30–2.33).

- Discusses use of service organizations (by client) and use of specialists (by auditor) (2.34–2.35).
- Materiality may require special consideration when excess of revenue over expense is designed to be very small (2.36).
- Additional client representations (2.43).
- Additional going-concern considerations (2.46).

CHAPTER 3—FINANCIAL STATEMENTS

- Financial statement titles: possible alternative titles (3.01, footnote 1).
- Guidance for inclusion of items in operating measure (3.12).
- For purposes of presentation of expenses by natural category, expenses included in other categories should be broken out (e.g., salaries included in cost of sales should be reported with salaries) (3.14).
- Organizations covered by guide but which do not meet SFAS No. 117 definition of NFP (see par. 1.04) are not required to functionalize expenses or present the functional/natural expense matrix, unless such organizations receive significant public contributions, in which case they must functionalize expenses (but need not present the matrix) (3.15).
- Operating cash flows do include agency transactions, even though these are not reported in the income statement (3.16).
- Receipt of cash restricted for acquisition of long-term assets is reported as a financing inflow and simultaneously as an investing outflow (even if still held in cash at year end, because that cash, being restricted, cannot be included with operating cash on the balance sheet) (3.18).

  —Such restricted cash is not considered a cash equivalent for purposes of the statement of cash flows, even though it meets the SFAS No. 95 definition (3.20).

- If comparative prior year information is summarized (i.e., does not include all required information by class), the titles of the financial statements and the footnotes must indicate that the information is summarized (3.21–3.22).
- Under SOP 94-3, an additional example of an economic interest is if the reporting entity has a right to or responsibility for the operating results of an affiliate (3.24).
- Noncompliance with donor-imposed restrictions (including failure to maintain an appropriate composition of assets to meet restrictions) should be disclosed if disclosure or accrual of a liability would be required by SFAS No. 5 (3.28).

CHAPTER 4—CASH

- Cash held for others should be reported as a separate line item (4.03).

CHAPTER 5—CONTRIBUTIONS

- Discussion of distinguishing agency from other transactions; factors to consider; examples (5.05–5.08, Table 5.1).

  —Discussion of how concept applies to federated fund-raisers; examples of how to present agency amounts in statement of income (5.09-5.10).
- Discussion of gifts-in-kind (5.11–5.13).

  —Gifts-in-kind contributed to be used in fund-raising events and which are subsequently sold at a profit should be recorded at fair value as contributions when received, and any additional amount received over the original fair value recorded as an additional contribution when sold (5.13).
- Costs of premiums sent to potential donors, and premiums of nominal value given to donors, are fund-raising expense (5.15).

—Factors to distinguish contributions from exchange transactions (5.17, Table 5.2).

—Discussion of distinction between membership dues and contributions; list of factors (5.18, Table 5.3).

- Timing of revenue recognition for membership dues (5.19).
- Resources received in exchange transactions are unrestricted, even though there may be legal or other restrictions associated with them (because the restrictions were not imposed by a *donor*) (5.22).
- Discussion of donor-imposed conditions; revenue recognition; examples (5.23–5.28).
- Discussion of donor-imposed restrictions (5.29 *et seq.*).

  —Unrestricted amounts used to match a restricted challenge grant become restricted (5.31).

  —If a long-lived asset that is implicitly restricted is sold, any gain or loss is unrestricted; any remaining temporarily restricted balance related to the asset should be reclassified (5.36).
- Promises to give (pledges):

  —An ultimate recipient of a gift through an agent should record an unconditional pledge when it learns that the agent has received the gift or pledge (5.39, footnote 14).

  —Discussion of what constitutes "sufficient verifiable evidence" to record a pledge (5.40).

  —Bequests should not be recorded until a will is declared valid (after death) (5.41).

  —Discussion of conditional pledges (5.41).
- Contributed services:

  —Should be recognized if employees of separately governed organizations perform services for and under the direction of the recipient organization (5.43).

  —Provision of free facilities and utilities should be recorded in the period used, except that an unconditional promise to continue to provide such use for an extended period should be recorded as temporarily restricted receivable and revenue (5.44).

—If a promise of use of a facility meets the criteria of SFAS No. 13 for a capital lease, it should be treated as such. If a facility is provided for below-market rent, the capitalization amount should be based on the fair rental value (5.44–5.45).

- Discussion of valuation of pledges of noncash gifts (5.48):

  —The recorded value of assets described in a conditional pledge should be determined based on their value when the condition is met (5.50).

  —If it is difficult to estimate what a noncash asset will be worth later when it is received, the current fair value may be the best estimate of the future value (5.51).

- Discounting and valuing pledges:

  —The discount should be reported as an offset to the receivable (5.51).

  —The recorded value of an asset described in an unconditional pledge should not be increased if the asset is worth more when transferred to the recipient, but should be decreased if the value is less (5.51).

  —The debit to initially establish an allowance for uncollectible pledges should be reported as bad debt expense in the net asset class in which the contribution revenue is reported (5.52). [Not specified: how to functionalize this expense.]

  —Subsequent changes in the allowance should be reported in the net asset class in which the contribution was initially reported or in the class in which the net assets are represented (5.52).

  —Interest rate used by recipient to compute discount is based solely on recipient's circumstances, not donor's (5.54).

  —Discount rate for a given pledge should not be changed after it is initially determined (5.54).

  —The interest method should be used to amortize discount; other methods may be used if not materially different (5.55).

- Financial statements:

  —Dues revenue may be reported as one line item; it may, but need not, be broken into portion representing true dues (exchange) and portion representing contribution (5.56).

  —Disclosures related to pledges receivable include gross pledges, present value discount, and allowance for uncollectibles, whether on the face or in notes (5.56).

  —Notes (5.57–5.58):

  (1) Accounting policies regarding:

  Implied time restriction on donated long-lived assets

  Reporting of restricted gifts when restriction is met in the same period as the gift is received

  Capitalization of collection items.

  (2) Disclosures:

  Pledged receivables;

  Aging schedule (less than one year, one to five years, more than five years) with related allowance and discount

  Conditional pledges, by category

  Those required by APB 21

  As to donated services: nature and extent of services received, activities conducted by volunteers, amount recorded.

  (3) Sample disclosures (5.59).

- Auditing:

  —Contributions receivable are not considered accounts receivable which must be confirmed (although auditor may decide to do so anyway).

CHAPTER 6—SPLIT-INTEREST GIFTS

- Extensive discussion of split-interest gifts (entire chapter).
- Irrevocable arrangements should be accounted for as part-gift, part-exchange transactions (6.04).

  —Assets received accounted for at fair value.

  —Contribution portion is revenue or gain.

—Liability related to the exchange portion (e.g., annuity liability to life tenant) is recorded.

- Not-for-profit organizations which are beneficiaries of arrangement should record it when they become aware of it (including arrangements where third parties hold the assets) (6.05).

  —If a third-party trustee has substantial discretion over distribution of the benefits of the arrangement, the arrangement is effectively conditional as to the charitable beneficiary, and would not be recorded until amounts due the beneficiary become unconditional.

- Revocable agreements are conditional; assets received in advance are offset by refundable advances; contribution revenue is recorded only when agreements become unconditional (6.06).

Accounting for Split Interests

- Initial recognition:

  —Revenue at fair value: (6.07)

  Lead agreement: present value of amounts to be received over life of agreement

  Remainder agreement: fair value of assets, less amounts due to life tenants (consider estimated return on assets, payment obligations [unstated factor: life expectancy of life tenants], discount rate).

  —Revenue is temporarily restricted unless donor has stipulated permanent restriction, or has indicated immediate availability to the charity of its interest in the assets (6.08).

  —When assets are held by independent third parties, the charity should record its beneficial interest in the assets (present value of estimated future distributions [which may be perpetual in some cases]) (6.10, 6.22–6.24).

- Recognition during the term of the agreement: (6.11)

  —Accretion of the discount that was initially applied to the contribution.

  —Revaluation of expected future benefits to be received.

—Revaluation of expected future payments to others (changes in life expectancy, etc.).

—When assets are held by the charity, income, gains, and losses should be reflected in the charity's accounts (6.12) [but, to the extent attributable to the life tenant, not reported in the financial statements (6.28)].

- Recognition at the termination of the arrangement: (6.15)

  —Remaining asset and liability accounts are closed to appropriate class of net assets.

  —Temporarily restricted amounts which are now available for unrestricted use are reclassified to the unrestricted class.

- Financial statements should separately disclose amounts related to split interest arrangements (6.15).

  —Note disclosures about existence and nature of agreements.

- When charity does not hold the assets, it recognizes its beneficial interest in the arrangement and changes in the value of that interest (6.21, 6.29).

- When charity is beneficiary of a perpetual third-party trust, it should record its interest as permanently restricted net assets (6.24).

  —Present value of estimated future receipts from trust may generally be measured by the fair value of the assets of the trust (6.24, footnote 6).

  —Periodic distributions are recorded as investment income (6.24).

- Under remainder interest arrangements, periodic income and payments to life tenants are recorded as changes in the asset and liability accounts, not as income and expense (6.28, 6.33, 6.37).

  —Adjustments for revaluation of assets and liabilities to reflect the passage of time and changes in actuarial assumptions (accretion of discount, changes in life expectancy, and actuarial gains or losses) are recorded as gains or losses (6.28, 6.33, 6.37)

- With a pooled income fund, the present value discount applied to the assets should be recorded as deferred revenue (6.36).

CHAPTER 7—OTHER ASSETS

- For contributions of inventory, when the items have no value (e.g., certain clothing and furniture that cannot be sold by the organization), the items should not be recognized (7.03).
- [Draft is silent about whether (when the donor is silent) there is an implied permanent restriction on *all* donations of collection items, and cash restricted for the acquisition of collection items, by virtue of the requirement in SFAS No. 116 that a condition for noncapitalization of collection items is the existence of an organizational policy limiting the use of proceeds from sale of collection items to the acquisition of other collection items. (If organization does not capitalize collection items, then this issue would only apply to cash donated for collection acquisition; if organization chooses to capitalize collection items, it would not be required to have the policy regarding disposals, but may nevertheless voluntarily adopt such a policy.)]

  —Sample disclosures relating to collection items (7.14).
- Discussion of auditing procedures applicable to noncapitalized collection items (7.16–7.18).

CHAPTER 8—INVESTMENTS

- Guide acknowledges FASB exposure draft on investments (March 1995), and requires investments covered by that draft to be accounted for at fair value (8.01). (See discussion of the final statement in Chapter 8 of this supplement.)
- Investments not covered by FASB draft should continue to be valued in accordance with whichever existing audit guide or SOP an organization is currently following (8.02, 8A.27–8A.29).

  If a guide requires all investments to be valued the same way, that rule applies only to investments not covered by the FASB draft (8.02).

- Organizations that do not meet the definition of a not-for-profit in SFAS No. 117 must follow the rules in SFAS No. 115 for reporting investments (8.06). (See also par. 1.04.)

CHAPTER 9—PROPERTY & EQUIPMENT

- Property acquired under grants and contracts, where the funder retains a residual right to reclaim the property at termination of the funding period, should be capitalized by the user of the property if it is probable that the organization will be allowed to keep the property (9.04).

  —Property capitalized in such circumstances should be disclosed.

- See par. 5.44 for discussion of contributions of the use of property (9.05).
- Depreciation should be recorded under SFAS No. 93 (9.07).

  Funders' regulations regarding charging of depreciation against grants or contracts should not affect financial reporting (9.07, footnote 4).

- When an organization's policy is to consider time restrictions on donated property to expire over the useful life of the property, the amount of the periodic reclassification need not equal the depreciation if the period over which the restriction is deemed to exist differs from the economic useful life of the property (9.08).

CHAPTER 10—DEBT AND OTHER LIABILITIES

- When a not-for-profit is responsible for tax-exempt debt issued by a government finance authority, the not-for-profit should include such debt on its balance sheet (10.02).
- The requirements of SFAS No. 109 on deferred taxes should be followed if applicable (excise tax on investment income of private foundations; unrelated business income tax) (10.03).

- Revenue received in advance in exchange transactions (e.g., preseason sale of theater tickets) should be deferred until earned (10.04).
- Discussion of recording of grants made to others; conditionality; when to record as a liability (parallel with grants receivable) (10.06).

CHAPTER 11—NET ASSETS

- Although use of the terms *unrestricted, temporarily restricted,* and *permanently restricted* is encouraged, it is not required; subdivisions of the classes are permitted on the face of the balance sheet (11.03, footnote 2).

  —Disclosure of different kinds of temporary and permanent restrictions should be disclosed either on the face or in a note (11.12).
- Donors may restrict individual assets as well as net assets (e.g., land restricted to use as a park) (11.04).

CHAPTER 12—REVENUES AND RECEIVABLES FROM EXCHANGE TRANSACTIONS

- The distinction between revenues and gains depends on each organization's circumstances; what is revenue to one may be a gain to another (12.03).
- Revenue from exchange transactions is unrestricted (12.04).
- Revenues and expenses must be reported gross, but directly related expenses may be shown as a deduction within the revenue section (e.g., cost of sales) (12.05, footnote 3).
- If the organization regularly provides certain services at a discount, or free, revenue should be reported net of the discount (reporting gross revenue, followed by the discount and a subtotal, is permitted) (12.05).

CHAPTER 13—EXPENSES, GAINS & LOSSES

- This guide will incorporate the guidance of either SOP 87-2 or its replacement 13.04, footnote 1).
- Expenses are unrestricted and may be segregated between operating and nonoperating if desired, per SFAS No. 117 (13.03).
- Expenses must be reported functionally, per SFAS No. 117, except for organizations that do not meet the definition of not-for-profit (see par. 1.04) (13.04–13.05).
- Fund-raising costs should be expensed currently, regardless of any hoped-for future economic benefit (13.07).

  —Fund-raising costs do not meet the criteria for deferral as advertising costs under SOP 93-7 (13.07, footnote 4).
- Direct-response advertising costs should be capitalized per SOP 93-7 (13.08):

  —Advertising includes solicitation of users for an organization's free services, but such costs cannot be capitalized beyond the first time the advertising takes place (13.09–13.10). [This would presumably allow deferral of costs to organize and create an advertising campaign prior to actually running the ad for the first time.]

  —Losses need not be functionalized (13.14).
- Discussion of distinction between expenses and losses (13.15–13.16).
- Cost of sales may be reported as a deduction from sales, or as an expense; if an expense, it must be functionalized according to its purpose, which may be program (e.g., museum bookstore) or supporting (e.g., cafeteria) (13.15).
- Revenue and expenses related to "special events" may be displayed as: (13.18–13.19)

  —Total gross revenue, with the cost of directly related goods and services provided:

  (1) as a line item deducted from the revenue, or

(2) shown in the same section of the statement as other expenses; or

—gross revenue may be allocated between the portion considered to be a contribution and the portion considered to be an exchange transaction, with the cost of the directly related goods and services shown as a line item deducted from the exchange revenue.

—direct costs include incremental costs of transactions with independent third parties and payroll costs of employees directly associated with the events (13.19).

- Guidance for distinguishing central and peripheral (per SFAC No. 6) events: (13.20)

  —Frequency and regularity.

  —Significance (relation to organization's budget).

- Investment management expenses that are netted against revenue (per SFAS No. 117) must be functionalized in the expense matrix if one is presented (13.22).
- Information about all expenses must be provided by function, regardless of where they are shown on the statement of activities; if not provided in an expense matrix, it may be in a note (13.24–13.25).

  —Sample notes (13.26).

- Disclose description of organization's major programs (13.29).
- Types of supporting services may be further disaggregated if desired (13.30).
- Management expenses include solicitation of revenue from exchange transactions (e.g., government contracts [not stated, but assumed to also cover advertising of goods and services sold by the organization, such as concert tickets]) 13.31).
- Costs of efforts to recruit volunteers are fund-raising expenses (13.32).
- Membership development costs may have to be allocated to more than one function: (13.33)

  —If dues are, in effect, partly or totally a contribution, costs are partly or wholly fund-raising.

- Discussion of allocation of costs (13.35–13.38).
- Occupancy and maintenance of property is not a functional category; these costs should be allocated to other categories (13.37).
- Interest cost should be allocated to specific functions to the extent possible; remaining interest cost is management expense (13.37).
- Payments to affiliates should be functionalized to the extent that it is practicable and reasonable to do so and the necessary information is available; unallocated amounts are a separate supporting service (13.40).
- All fund-raising activities of federated fund-raising organizations are reported as fund-raising expenses (13.41).

CHAPTER 14—AUDITORS' REPORTS

- The opinion paragraph should refer to "changes in net assets" rather than results of operations, even if an operating subtotal is presented (14.02).
- If comparative financial information does not include all required disclosures, the report should include a paragraph describing that fact; the paragraph should not affect, or be referred to in, the scope or opinion paragraphs (14.05; see also pars. 3.21–3.22).
- Nonmonetary information (e.g., statistics about the organization's programs) should not be included in the statements or notes; if it is, it should be marked unaudited and the auditor should not comment on it (14.10).
- If financial statements are prepared on a basis of accounting required by a governmental regulatory agency that is not GAAP and not an OCBOA, the auditor may issue a special report under SAS No. 62; the report must include a paragraph restricting distribution of the report to the client and the agency (even if, by law, the financial statements are a matter of public record) (14.12).

CHAPTER 15—TAX CONSIDERATIONS

- General discussion of tax matters relevant to not-for-profits; auditor's responsibility for assessing organization's tax status and compliance.

CHAPTER 16—FUND ACCOUNTING

- Discussion of allocating funds into classes of net assets.
- The portion of loan fund balances which represents a refundable advance (e.g., under a government loan program) should be reported as a liability (16.12).

Bibliography

p. 651. ***Replace fifth item with:***

Auditing Standards Division, "Compliance Auditing Considerations in Audits of Governmental Entities and Recipients of Governmental Financial Assistance," Statement on Auditing Standards No. 74, 1995.

p. 651. ***Add at end of seventh item:***

Exposure draft issued in 1995 (see Appendix D of this supplement).

p. 652. ***Add to first item:***

Exposure draft of new audit guide issued in 1995.

p. 652. ***Add to list under Financial Accounting Standards Board:***

SFAS No. 124: "Accounting for Certain Investments Held by Not-for-Profit Organizations," 1995.

Exposure Draft: "Consolidated Financial Statements: Policy and Procedures," 1995.

Exposure Draft: "Proposed Interpretation: Transfers of Assets in Which a Not-for-Profit Organization Acts as an Agent, Trustee, or Intermediary (an Interpretation of FASB Statement No. 116)," 1995.

p. 652. ***Move Evangelical Joint Accounting Committee above Financial Accounting Standards Board.***

p. 652. ***Add to Evangelical Joint Accounting Committee entry:***

The new edition was published in late 1994.

p. 653. ***Add to National Health Council entry:***

4th edition is to be published in 1996.

p. 654. ***Add to last item:***

8th edition to be published in 1996.

Supplement Index